The New York Times

IN THE HEADLINES

#MeToo

WOMEN SPEAK OUT AGAINST SEXUAL ASSAULT

THE NEW YORK TIMES EDITORIAL STAFF

Published in 2019 by New York Times Educational Publishing
in association with The Rosen Publishing Group, Inc.
29 East 21st Street, New York, NY 10010

First Edition

The New York Times
Alex Ward: Editorial Director, Book Development
Brenda Hutchings: Senior Photo Editor/Art Buyer
Phyllis Collazo: Photo Rights/Permissions Editor
Heidi Giovine: Administrative Manager

Rosen Publishing
Jacob R. Steinberg: Director of Content Development
Greg Tucker: Creative Director
Brian Garvey: Art Director

Cataloging-in-Publication Data
Names: New York Times Company.
Title: #MeToo: women speak out against sexual assault / edited
by the New York Times editorial staff.
Description: New York : New York Times Educational Publishing,
2019. | Series: In the headlines | Includes bibliographic refer-
ences and index.
Identifiers: ISBN 9781642820027 (pbk.) | ISBN 9781642820010
(library bound) | ISBN 9781642820003 (ebook)
Subjects: LCSH: Sexual harassment of women—Juvenile literature.
| Sexual harassment—Juvenile literature. | Sexual harassment of
women—Juvenile literature. | Women—Crimes against—Juvenile
literature. | Social movements—Juvenile literature.
Classification: LCC HV6250.4.W65 M486 2019 | DDC 362.883—dc23

Manufactured in the United States of America

On the cover: Illustration by The New York Times

Contents

CHAPTER 4

Criticism of the #MeToo Movement

What's Next?

Introduction

IT STARTED WITH A TWEET: "If you've been sexually harassed or assaulted write 'me too' as a reply to this tweet." But the groundwork for #MeToo was laid more than twenty years earlier, and the conditions for the outpouring of support have existed for generations. #MeToo has grown into a worldwide catalyst for changes in the ways people think about, respond to and deal with sexual misconduct.

Social activist and community organizer Tarana Burke was at a loss for words in 1997 when a 13-year-old girl named Heaven told her about the sexual abuse she suffered at the hands of her mother's boyfriend. Ms. Burke later wished she had said, "Me too." Nine years later, Ms. Burke devised the Me Too campaign to draw attention to the pervasive problem of sexual assault and harassment in conjunction with an organization she founded, Just Be Inc., to promote the health and wellness of young female minorities.

Twenty-one years later, nothing much had changed. Millions of women and girls were still subjected to sexual abuse, assault and harassment, and few perpetrators were caught or punished. And then actress Alyssa Milano sent out the tweet that would start a revolution. Inspired by The New York Times's reports of the powerful Hollywood director Harvey Weinstein's habitual harassment and assault of young women over the course of his thirty-year career, Ms. Milano started the #MeToo social media hashtag on October 15, 2017, inviting women to publicly declare their membership in a group to which no one wanted to belong, but to which so many people do.

The #MeToo movement spread. In Canada, the movement initiated proposals to change sexual harassment laws. The French government considered issuing fines for catcalls. The people of India, Argentina

Activist Tarana Burke speaks at the #MeToo Survivors March & Rally on Nov. 12, 2017, in Hollywood, California.

and Uruguay, countries that have recently tightened their laws against sexual aggression, reflected on the reality that it is easier to change laws than it is behavior. In the United States, the #MeToo movement served as the impetus for other new movements, including Time's Up, an organization dedicated in part to providing legal advocacy for women who face sexual harassment in the workplace.

The huge number of responses to #MeToo led to the public pronouncement of guilt and the resignations of dozens of high-profile men, including actors, directors, newscasters, politicians and corporate executives. The swift downfall of so many men as a result of the accusations levied by those involved in the #MeToo movement led some people to question the lack of due process for the accused. Actor Matt Damon and novelist Margaret Atwood faced a backlash for voicing concerns about the extremism of the movement. Mr. Damon pointed out the dangers of not distinguishing the difference between inappropriate touching and rape. Ms. Atwood questioned the fate of a society that bypasses the legal system in pursuit of justice. Both were compelled by numerous angry responses to their statements to apologize for their positions.

The overall success of the #MeToo movement lies less with short-term victories and more with long-term results in motivating cultural, political and legal change in how sexual misconduct is managed, reported and penalized. #MeToo has the potential to change the world.

CHAPTER 1

The Start of the #MeToo Movement

Sexual harassment is not new, nor is it uncommon or hidden. What is new, however, is social media. When The New York Times exposed movie producer Harvey Weinstein's chronic sexual harassment of women, the social media hashtag #MeToo was born and went viral, kicking into high gear an existing movement to raise awareness about the prevalence of this type of behavior.

Harvey Weinstein Paid Off Sexual Harassment Accusers for Decades

BY JODI KANTOR AND MEGAN TWOHEY | OCT. 5, 2017

TWO DECADES AGO, the Hollywood producer Harvey Weinstein invited Ashley Judd to the Peninsula Beverly Hills hotel for what the young actress expected to be a business breakfast meeting. Instead, he had her sent up to his room, where he appeared in a bathrobe and asked if he could give her a massage or she could watch him shower, she recalled in an interview.

"How do I get out of the room as fast as possible without alienating Harvey Weinstein?" Ms. Judd said she remembers thinking.

In 2014, Mr. Weinstein invited Emily Nestor, who had worked just one day as a temporary employee, to the same hotel and made another offer: If she accepted his sexual advances, he would boost her career, according to accounts she provided to colleagues who sent them to

Weinstein Company executives. The following year, once again at the Peninsula, a female assistant said Mr. Weinstein badgered her into giving him a massage while he was naked, leaving her "crying and very distraught," wrote a colleague, Lauren O'Connor, in a searing memo asserting sexual harassment and other misconduct by their boss.

"There is a toxic environment for women at this company," Ms. O'Connor said in the letter, addressed to several executives at the company run by Mr. Weinstein.

An investigation by The New York Times found previously undisclosed allegations against Mr. Weinstein stretching over nearly three decades, documented through interviews with current and former employees and film industry workers, as well as legal records, emails and internal documents from the businesses he has run, Miramax and the Weinstein Company.

During that time, after being confronted with allegations including sexual harassment and unwanted physical contact, Mr. Weinstein has reached at least eight settlements with women, according to two company officials speaking on the condition of anonymity. Among the recipients, The Times found, were a young assistant in New York in 1990, an actress in 1997, an assistant in London in 1998, an Italian model in 2015 and Ms. O'Connor shortly after, according to records and those familiar with the agreements.

In a statement to The Times on Thursday afternoon, Mr. Weinstein said: "I appreciate the way I've behaved with colleagues in the past has caused a lot of pain, and I sincerely apologize for it. Though I'm trying to do better, I know I have a long way to go."

He added that he was working with therapists and planning to take a leave of absence to "deal with this issue head on."

Lisa Bloom, a lawyer advising Mr. Weinstein, said in a statement that "he denies many of the accusations as patently false." In comments to The Times earlier this week, Mr. Weinstein said that many claims in Ms. O'Connor's memo were "off base" and that they had parted on good terms.

He and his representatives declined to comment on any of the settlements, including providing information about who paid them. But Mr. Weinstein said that in addressing employee concerns about workplace issues, "my motto is to keep the peace."

Ms. Bloom, who has been advising Mr. Weinstein over the last year on gender and power dynamics, called him "an old dinosaur learning new ways." She said she had "explained to him that due to the power difference between a major studio head like him and most others in the industry, whatever his motives, some of his words and behaviors can be perceived as inappropriate, even intimidating."

Though Ms. O'Connor had been writing only about a two-year period, her memo echoed other women's complaints. Mr. Weinstein required her to have casting discussions with aspiring actresses after they had private appointments in his hotel room, she said, her description matching those of other former employees. She suspected that she and other female Weinstein employees, she wrote, were being used to facilitate liaisons with "vulnerable women who hope he will get them work."

The allegations piled up even as Mr. Weinstein helped define popular culture. He has collected six best-picture Oscars and turned out a number of touchstones, from the films "Sex, Lies, and Videotape," "Pulp Fiction" and "Good Will Hunting" to the television show "Project Runway." In public, he presents himself as a liberal lion, a champion of women and a winner of not just artistic but humanitarian awards.

In 2015, the year Ms. O'Connor wrote her memo, his company distributed "The Hunting Ground," a documentary about campus sexual assault. A longtime Democratic donor, he hosted a fund-raiser for Hillary Clinton in his Manhattan home last year. He employed Malia Obama, the oldest daughter of former President Barack Obama, as an intern this year, and recently helped endow a faculty chair at Rutgers University in Gloria Steinem's name. During the Sundance Film Festival in January, when Park City, Utah, held its version of nationwide women's marches, Mr. Weinstein joined the parade.

"From the outside, it seemed golden — the Oscars, the success, the remarkable cultural impact," said Mark Gill, former president of Miramax Los Angeles when the company was owned by Disney. "But behind the scenes, it was a mess, and this was the biggest mess of all," he added, referring to Mr. Weinstein's treatment of women.

Dozens of Mr. Weinstein's former and current employees, from assistants to top executives, said they knew of inappropriate conduct while they worked for him. Only a handful said they ever confronted him.

Mr. Weinstein enforced a code of silence; employees of the Weinstein Company have contracts saying they will not criticize it or its leaders in a way that could harm its "business reputation" or "any employee's personal reputation," a recent document shows. And most of the women accepting payouts agreed to confidentiality clauses prohibiting them from speaking about the deals or the events that led to them.

Charles Harder, a lawyer representing Mr. Weinstein, said it was not unusual to enter into settlements to avoid lengthy and costly litigation. He added, "It's not evidence of anything."

At Fox News, where the conservative icons Roger E. Ailes and Bill O'Reilly were accused of harassment, women have received payouts well into the millions of dollars. But most of the women involved in the Weinstein agreements collected between roughly $80,000 and $150,000, according to people familiar with the negotiations.

In the wake of Ms. O'Connor's 2015 memo, some Weinstein Company board members and executives, including Mr. Weinstein's brother and longtime partner, Bob, 62, were alarmed about the allegations, according to several people who spoke on the condition of anonymity. In the end, though, board members were assured there was no need to investigate. After reaching a settlement with Mr. Weinstein, Ms. O'Connor withdrew her complaint and thanked him for the career opportunity he had given her.

"The parties made peace very quickly," Ms. Bloom said.

Through her lawyer, Nicole Page, Ms. O'Connor declined to be interviewed. In the memo, she explained how unnerved she was by what she witnessed or encountered while a literary scout and production executive at the company. "I am just starting out in my career, and have been and remain fearful about speaking up," Ms. O'Connor wrote. "But remaining silent is causing me great distress."

In speaking out about her hotel episode, Ms. Judd said in a recent interview, "Women have been talking about Harvey amongst ourselves for a long time, and it's simply beyond time to have the conversation publicly."

A COMMON NARRATIVE

Ms. Nestor, a law and business school student, accepted Mr. Weinstein's breakfast invitation at the Peninsula because she did not want to miss an opportunity, she later told colleagues. After she arrived, he offered to help her career while boasting about a series of famous actresses he claimed to have slept with, according to accounts that colleagues compiled after hearing her story and then sent on to company executives.

"She said he was very persistent and focused though she kept saying no for over an hour," one internal document said. Ms. Nestor, who declined to comment for this article, refused his bargain, the records noted. "She was disappointed that he met with her and did not seem to be interested in her résumé or skill set." The young woman chose not to report the episode to human resources personnel, but the allegations came to management's attention through other employees.

Across the years and continents, accounts of Mr. Weinstein's conduct share a common narrative: Women reported to a hotel for what they thought were work reasons, only to discover that Mr. Weinstein, who has been married for most of three decades, sometimes seemed to have different interests. His home base was New York, but his rolling headquarters were luxury hotels: the Peninsula Beverly Hills and the Savoy in London, the Hôtel du Cap-Eden-Roc near the Cannes Film Festival in France and the Stein Eriksen Lodge near the Sundance Film Festival.

Working for Mr. Weinstein could mean getting him out of bed in the morning and doing "turndown duty" late at night, preparing him for sleep. Like the colleague cited in Ms. O'Connor's memo, some junior employees required to perform those tasks said they were disturbing.

In interviews, eight women described varying behavior by Mr. Weinstein: appearing nearly or fully naked in front of them, requiring them to be present while he bathed or repeatedly asking for a massage or initiating one himself. The women, typically in their early or middle 20s and hoping to get a toehold in the film industry, said he could switch course quickly — meetings and clipboards one moment, intimate comments the next. One woman advised a peer to wear a parka when summoned for duty as a layer of protection against unwelcome advances.

Laura Madden, a former employee who said Mr. Weinstein prodded her for massages at hotels in Dublin and London beginning in 1991, said he had a way of making anyone who objected feel like an outlier. "It was so manipulative," she said in an interview. "You constantly question yourself — am I the one who is the problem?"

"I don't know anything about that," Mr. Weinstein said.

Most women who told The Times that they experienced misconduct by Mr. Weinstein had never met one another. They range in age from early 20s to late 40s and live in different cities. Some said they did not report the behavior because there were no witnesses and they feared retaliation by Mr. Weinstein. Others said they felt embarrassed. But most confided in co-workers.

Ms. Madden later told Karen Katz, a friend and colleague in the acquisitions department, about Mr. Weinstein's overtures, including a time she locked herself in the bathroom of his hotel room, sobbing. "We were so young at the time," said Ms. Katz, now a documentary filmmaker. "We did not understand how wrong it was or how Laura should deal with it."

Others in the London office said the same. "I was pretty disturbed and angry," said Sallie Hodges, another former employee, recalling the accounts she heard from colleagues. "That's kind of the way things were."

The human resources operation was considered weak in New York and worse in London, so some employees banded together in solidarity. "If a female executive was asked to go to a meeting solo, she and a colleague would generally double up" so as not to be alone with Mr. Weinstein, recalled Mr. Gill, the former president of Miramax Los Angeles.

Many women who worked with Mr. Weinstein said they never experienced sexual harassment or knew of anyone who did, and recalled him as a boss who gave them valuable opportunities at young ages. Some described long and satisfying careers with him, praising him as a mentor and advocate.

But in interviews, some of the former employees who said they had troubling experiences with Mr. Weinstein asked a common question: How could allegations repeating the same pattern — young women, a powerful male producer, even some of the same hotels — have accumulated for almost three decades?

"It wasn't a secret to the inner circle," said Kathy DeClesis, Bob Weinstein's assistant in the early 1990s. She supervised a young woman who left the company abruptly after an encounter with Harvey Weinstein and who later received a settlement, according to several former employees.

Speaking up could have been costly. A job with Mr. Weinstein was a privileged perch at the nexus of money, fame and art, and plenty of his former assistants have risen high in Hollywood. He could be charming and generous: gift baskets, flowers, personal or career help and cash. At the Cannes Film Festival, according to several former colleagues, he sometimes handed out thousands of dollars as impromptu bonuses.

Mr. Weinstein was a volcanic personality, though, given to fits of rage and personal lashings of male and female employees alike. When a female guest of his had to wait for a hotel room upgrade, he yelled that Ms. O'Connor would be better off marrying a "fat, rich Jewish" man because she was probably just good for "being a wife" and "making babies," she wrote in her memo. (He added some expletives, she said.) His treatment of women was sometimes written off as just another form of toxicity, according to multiple former employees.

In the fall of 1998, a 25-year-old London assistant named Zelda Perkins confronted Mr. Weinstein. According to former colleagues, she and several co-workers had been regularly subjected to inappropriate requests or comments in hotel rooms, and she was particularly concerned about the treatment of another woman in the office. She told Mr. Weinstein that he had to stop, according to the former colleagues, and that she would go public or initiate legal action unless he changed his behavior.

Steve Hutensky, one of Miramax's entertainment lawyers, was dispatched to London to negotiate a settlement with Ms. Perkins and her lawyer. He declined to comment for this article.

Ms. Perkins, now a theater producer in London, also declined to comment for this article, saying that she could not discuss her work at Miramax or whether she had entered into any agreements.

Months after the settlement, Mr. Weinstein triumphed at the Oscars, with "Life Is Beautiful" and "Shakespeare in Love" winning 10 awards. A few years later, Mr. Weinstein, who had produced a series of British-themed movies, was made a Commander of the British Empire, an honorary title just short of knighthood.

'COERCIVE BARGAINING'

For actors, a meeting with Mr. Weinstein could yield dazzling rewards: scripts, parts, award campaigns, magazine coverage, influence on lucrative endorsement deals. He knew how to blast small films to box office success, and deliver polished dramas like "The King's Speech" and popular attractions like the "Scary Movie" franchise. Mr. Weinstein's films helped define femininity, sex and romance, from Catherine Zeta-Jones in "Chicago" to Jennifer Lawrence in "Silver Linings Playbook."

But movies were also his private leverage. When Mr. Weinstein invited Ms. Judd to breakfast in Beverly Hills, she had been shooting the thriller "Kiss the Girls" all night, but the meeting seemed too important to miss. After arriving at the hotel lobby, she was surprised to learn that they would be talking in his suite; she decided to order cereal, she said, so the food would come quickly and she could leave.

Mr. Weinstein soon issued invitation after invitation, she said. Could he give her a massage? When she refused, he suggested a shoulder rub. She rejected that too, she recalled. He steered her toward a closet, asking her to help pick out his clothing for the day, and then toward the bathroom. Would she watch him take a shower? she remembered him saying.

"I said no, a lot of ways, a lot of times, and he always came back at me with some new ask," Ms. Judd said. "It was all this bargaining, this coercive bargaining."

To get out of the room, she said, she quipped that if Mr. Weinstein wanted to touch her, she would first have to win an Oscar in one of his movies. She recalled feeling "panicky, trapped," she said in the interview. "There's a lot on the line, the cachet that came with Miramax."

Not long afterward, she related what had happened to her mother, the singer Naomi Judd, who confirmed their conversation to a Times reporter. Years later, Ashley Judd appeared in two Weinstein films without incident, she said. In 2015, she shared an account of the episode in the hotel room with Variety without naming the man involved.

In 1997, Mr. Weinstein reached a previously undisclosed settlement with Rose McGowan, then a 23-year-old-actress, after an episode in a hotel room during the Sundance Film Festival. The $100,000 settlement was "not to be construed as an admission" by Mr. Weinstein, but intended to "avoid litigation and buy peace," according to the legal document, which was reviewed by The Times. Ms. McGowan had just appeared in the slasher film "Scream" and would later star in the television show "Charmed." She declined to comment.

INCREASED SCRUTINY

Just months before Ms. O'Connor wrote her memo, a young female employee quit after complaining of being forced to arrange what she believed to be assignations for Mr. Weinstein, according to two people familiar with her departure. The woman, who asked not to be identified to protect her privacy, said a nondisclosure agreement prevented her from commenting.

Soon, complaints about Mr. Weinstein's behavior prompted the board of his company to take notice.

In March 2015, Mr. Weinstein had invited Ambra Battilana, an Italian model and aspiring actress, to his TriBeCa office on a Friday evening to discuss her career. Within hours, she called the police. Ms. Battilana told them that Mr. Weinstein had grabbed her breasts after asking if they were real and put his hands up her skirt, the police report says.

The claims were taken up by the New York Police Department's Special Victims Squad and splashed across the pages of tabloids, along with reports that the woman had worked with investigators to secretly record a confession from Mr. Weinstein. The Manhattan district attorney's office later declined to bring charges.

But Mr. Weinstein made a payment to Ms. Battilana, according to people familiar with the settlement, speaking on the condition of anonymity about the confidential agreement.

The public nature of the episode concerned some executives and board members of the Weinstein Company. (Harvey and Bob Weinstein together own 42 percent of the privately held business.) When several board members pressed Mr. Weinstein about it, he insisted that the woman had set him up, colleagues recalled.

Ms. Battilana had testified in court proceedings against associates of former Prime Minister Silvio Berlusconi of Italy who are accused of procuring women for alleged sex parties, and the Italian news media also reported that, years ago, Ms. Battilana accused a septuagenarian boyfriend of sexual harassment, a complaint that was apparently dismissed. Ms. Battilana did not respond to requests for comment. Her lawyer, Mauro Rufini, could not be reached for comment.

After the episode, Lance Maerov, a board member, said he successfully pushed for a code of behavior for the company that included detailed language about sexual harassment.

Then Ms. O'Connor's memo hit, with page after page of detailed accusations. In describing the experiences of women at the company, including her own, she wrote, "The balance of power is me: 0, Harvey Weinstein: 10."

She was a valued employee — Mr. Weinstein described her as "fantastic," "a great person," "a brilliant executive" — so the complaint rattled top executives, including Bob Weinstein. When the board was notified of it by email, Mr. Maerov insisted that an outside lawyer determine whether the allegations were true, he said in an interview.

But the inquiry never happened. Mr. Weinstein had reached a settlement with Ms. O'Connor, and there was no longer anything to investigate.

"Because this matter has been resolved and no further action is required, I withdraw my complaint," Ms. O'Connor wrote in an email to the head of human resources six days after sending her memo. She also wrote a letter to Mr. Weinstein thanking him for the opportunity to learn about the entertainment industry.

RACHEL ABRAMS AND WILLIAM K. RASHBAUM CONTRIBUTED REPORTING. GRACE ASHFORD CONTRIBUTED RESEARCH.

Statement From Harvey Weinstein

BY HARVEY WEINSTEIN | OCT. 5, 2017

Harvey Weinstein sent The Times the following statement in response to our story about his treatment of women in Hollywood. In the article's aftermath, actresses spoke out, politicians distanced themselves and an adviser called his behavior "gross."

I CAME OF AGE in the 60's and 70's, when all the rules about behavior and workplaces were different. That was the culture then.

I have since learned it's not an excuse, in the office — or out of it. To anyone.

I realized some time ago that I needed to be a better person and my interactions with the people I work with have changed.

I appreciate the way I've behaved with colleagues in the past has caused a lot of pain, and I sincerely apologize for it.

Though I'm trying to do better, I know I have a long way to go. That is my commitment. My journey now will be to learn about myself and conquer my demons. Over the last year I've asked Lisa Bloom to tutor me and she's put together a team of people. I've brought on therapists and I plan to take a leave of absence from my company and to deal with this issue head on. I so respect all women and regret what happened. I hope that my actions will speak louder than words and that one day we will all be able to earn their trust and sit down together with Lisa to learn more. Jay Z wrote in 4:44 "I'm not the man I thought I was and I better be that man for my children." The same is true for me. I want a second chance in the community but I know I've got work to do to earn it. I have goals that are now priorities. Trust me, this isn't an overnight process. I've been trying to do this for 10 years and this is a wake-up call. I cannot be more remorseful about the people I hurt and I plan to do right by all of them.

I am going to need a place to channel that anger so I've decided that I'm going to give the NRA my full attention. I hope Wayne LaPierre

Harvey Weinstein, who faces accusations of sexual harassment stretching back decades, is the driving force behind the Weinstein Company.

will enjoy his retirement party. I'm going to do it at the same place I had my Bar Mitzvah. I'm making a movie about our President, perhaps we can make it a joint retirement party. One year ago, I began organizing a $5 million foundation to give scholarships to women directors at USC. While this might seem coincidental, it has been in the works for a year. It will be named after my mom and I won't disappoint her.

Harvey Weinstein's Fall Opens the Floodgates in Hollywood

BY JIM RUTENBERG, RACHEL ABRAMS AND MELENA RYZIK | OCT. 16, 2017

LOS ANGELES — Harvey Weinstein is certainly not the first powerful man publicly and credibly accused of sexually harassing or abusing women in recent years.

Since 2015, the Fox News chairman Roger Ailes, the Fox News prime-time host Bill O'Reilly and the comedian and actor Bill Cosby have suffered professional, financial or reputational setbacks after numerous women told stories of their sexual misconduct.

Those stories dominated news cycles, to be sure, but the outcry accompanying Mr. Weinstein's downfall seems louder and more impassioned — perhaps because Mr. Weinstein's accusers include stars like Ashley Judd, Angelina Jolie and Gwyneth Paltrow.

"I think this is a watershed moment," said the producer Gail Berman, who had top jobs at Paramount Pictures and the Fox network.

That became clear on Sunday, when Facebook, Instagram and Twitter were flooded with messages from women who used the hashtag #MeToo to acknowledge that they had dealt with sexual harassment or assault. A tweet posted by the actress Alyssa Milano inspired the online campaign.

"If you've been sexually harassed or assaulted write 'me too' as a reply to this tweet," Ms. Milano wrote.

Twitter promoted the #MeToo campaign on Moments, its platform of highlighted stories, and the hashtag went on to be used more than 500,000 times in its first 24 hours by people from all lines of work. Those taking part included the singer Lady Gaga; the actresses Rosario Dawson, Anna Paquin and Evan Rachel Wood; and the poet Najwa Zebian.

The Oscar-winning director Kathryn Bigelow applauded the movement. "The democratization of the spread of information can finally move faster than a powerful media mogul's attempts to bury it," she said by email.

In recent days, the singer Bjork, the "Riverdale" actress Lili Reinhart and the "Inside Edition" correspondent Lisa Guerrero lodged new accusations against other men who work in entertainment.

The singer and actress Courtney Love accused the powerful Creative Artists Agency of punishing her after she raised questions about Mr. Weinstein's behavior in 2005, and a recently unearthed video clip of Ms. Love making the charge has gone viral.

The model Cameron Russell started a thread on her Instagram account on misconduct by men in fashion. It has led to more than 50 models anonymously sharing their stories of harassment.

Kicked off by reports on the allegations against Mr. Weinstein, the outpouring came a little more than a year after The Washington Post published leaked excerpts from an "Access Hollywood" tape in which Donald J. Trump, then a candidate for president, boasted of groping women.

At issue now is whether or not Hollywood can continue its old way of doing business, with self-styled "outlaw" executives and auteurs getting away with sexual misconduct as lawyers and publicists protect them.

"I think it's upsetting and devastating, all of the stories that have come out," said Nina Jacobson, a film producer who was formerly the president of the Walt Disney Company's Buena Vista Motion Pictures Group. "But I think the floodgates being opened is something that had to happen and that finally brings a subject to the surface that has sort of gone unchecked for countless years."

Beginning with an article about the allegations against Mr. Weinstein that The New York Times published on Oct. 5, more than 30 accusers have stepped forward with charges of harassment, assault and even rape against the mogul. The police in New York and London have started criminal investigations. (Mr. Weinstein has denied engaging in nonconsensual sex.)

Fatima Goss Graves, president and chief executive of the National Women's Law Center, said that, since the story broke, "we've gotten twice the volume of calls of people who have said they've experienced harassment."

The reaction has also led some senior women in Hollywood to predict that their longtime calls for change may finally come to something.

"I don't think this is going back to the status quo," said Ms. Berman, the producer. "You'll see that there will be improvement."

The industry took a step toward that on Monday, when the Producers Guild of America moved to terminate Mr. Weinstein's membership and issued a statement that seemed to catch up with the wave of disapproval sweeping social media.

"Sexual harassment of any type is completely unacceptable," it said in part. "This is a systemic and pervasive problem requiring immediate industrywide action."

On Saturday, the board of the Academy of Motion Picture Arts and Sciences stripped Mr. Weinstein of his academy membership. The move drew ridicule from the HBO comedy host John Oliver, given that it did no such thing in the cases of Mr. Cosby and Roman Polanski, who, in 1977, pleaded guilty to having unlawful sex with a 13-year-old girl and then fled the country.

"So congratulations, Hollywood," Mr. Oliver said. "See you at the next Oscars, where — and this is true — Casey Affleck will be presenting Best Actress."

The reference was cutting: Mr. Affleck, who won the best actor award at this year's Oscars for "Manchester by the Sea," had settled sexual harassment allegations made against him by two female producers in civil suits. He has denied the accusations.

Woody Allen served as the imperfect messenger for those cautioning against what he termed a "witch hunt." His warning was in line with the thinking of some executives, who said they were wary of false accusations getting easy play on social media.

In breaking the news about the allegations, The Times and The New Yorker carefully corroborated women's stories. Social media has no such checks and balances.

A spreadsheet listing men in the media business accused of sexist behaviors ranging from inappropriate flirting to rape surfaced last week and was circulated by email. The BuzzFeed writer Doree Shafrir weighed in on the list, writing of men who were said to be guilty of behaviors like leering: "Things do get complicated when you start lumping all this behavior together in a big anonymous spreadsheet of unsubstantiated allegations against dozens of named men."

Ms. Jacobson, the film producer, said, "There's an importance to a careful vetting and a careful reposting and not just a free-for-all." She added that she was in favor of more information, not less, which is why, she said, the industry has to tackle the use of nondisclosure agreements.

"It clearly feels like we have to take the burden away from people to come forward," she said. "They should not fear that, because you have an NDA, that you can't speak up."

Each successive case of a powerful man's misdeeds bursting into the open helps to embolden the next round, the feminist Gloria Steinem said.

"When dealing with deep bias like racism and sexism, it usually takes more than one injustice — or even a few," Ms. Steinem wrote in an email. "The Weinstein scandal would probably have been taken less seriously if Cosby, Ailes and others hadn't come first and been within easy memory."

Melinda McGillivray, who stepped forward last year to accuse Mr. Trump of groping her at his Mar-a-Lago club in Florida in 2003, told BuzzFeed last week that Ms. Paltrow and Ms. Jolie had an impact her accusation did not because of their star power. (Mr. Trump has denied harassment accusations.)

Mr. Trump's election had put some women here on guard against a return to male misbehavior that was more common 40 years ago. And one list circulating among ranking female executives in the industry has tracked a string of promotions of men to senior jobs — at Apple and AMC, Sony and Hulu, Fox and CBS — amid fear that progress for women has stalled since November.

"Most of the available senior management television jobs this year have gone to men," said Katie O'Connell, a chief executive of Platform One Media, and formerly the chief executive of Gaumont Television. "While those men were all qualified, it does highlight diminished access for these highest-level positions for women in 2017."

As part of the general reaction to the articles on Mr. Weinstein, the Hollywood & Highland shopping center removed from its 17-year-old "Road to Hollywood" public art exhibit a daybed that some have taken to represent the proverbial "casting couch" — the symbol of ritualized abuse that studio chiefs meted out in trading roles for sexual favors. It was removed because it had "attracted increased public attention and it has been threatened with damage," a spokeswoman for the mall said.

The artist behind the installation, Erika Rothenberg, said in an interview that her work was not meant to invoke the casting couch. Referring to Mr. Weinstein's case, she said she was "completely sympathetic to people who have feelings about this, who are angry about this."

Nonetheless, she said she hoped the daybed would return. "I don't think this piece is the problem," Ms. Rothenberg said.

#MeToo Floods Social Media With Stories of Harassment and Assault

BY ANNA CODREA-RADO | OCT. 16, 2017

WOMEN ARE posting messages on social media to show how commonplace sexual assault and harassment are, using the hashtag #MeToo to express that they, too, have been victims of such misconduct.

The messages bearing witness began appearing frequently on Twitter, Facebook and Instagram on Sunday, when the actress Alyssa Milano posted a screenshot outlining the idea and writing "If you've been sexually harassed or assaulted write 'me too' as a reply to this tweet."

Tens of thousands of people replied to the message. Some just wrote "me too," while many others described their personal experiences of harassment or assault.

The author and poet Najwa Zebian wrote: "I was blamed for it. I was told not to talk about it. I was told that it wasn't that bad. I was told to get over it."

Other celebrities who took part include Anna Paquin, Debra Messing, Laura Dreyfuss, Lady Gaga and Evan Rachel Wood.

Men also expressed their support. The comedian and activist Nick Jack Pappas wrote: "Men, Don't say you have a mother, a sister, a daughter... Say you have a father, a brother, a son who can do better. We all can."

Since The New York Times published an investigative report on Oct. 5 detailing decades of sexual harassment allegations against the Hollywood producer Harvey Weinstein, social media has provided a galvanizing platform for women to discuss their experiences.

Twitter bolstered the #MeToo trend by promoting it on Moments, its platform of curated stories.

The company pointed to its statement from last week in which it said it was "proud to empower and support the voices on our platform,

Actress Evan Rachel Wood was one of many celebrities who responded to #MeToo.

especially those that speak truth to power." It also noted that its chief executive, Jack Dorsey, had tweeted about the company's efforts to tackle abuse on the site.

The #MeToo movement is not the first to use social media to highlight abuse against women. In 2014, a #YesAllWomen campaign drew notice on social media after a man cited his hatred of women as his reason for killing people in Southern California. The activist Laura Bates started the #EverydaySexism campaign in 2012 to document widespread sexism, harassment and assault.

The Raw Power of #MeToo

OPINION | BY MARGARET RENKL | OCT. 19, 2017

A FEW YEARS BACK, when there were still three teenagers in this house, I got a little wound up at supper one night and kept going on and on about the brilliance of a novel I was reading by an Irish-born writer. "I can't believe you've never been there," one of my sons said. "As much as you love this stuff, I can't believe you've never been to Ireland or England."

"Well, it's expensive," I said. "First I had no money, and then I had a bunch of kids. And y'all need shoes more than I need Ireland. I'll get there one day."

The skeptical teen was not satisfied with this answer. "Dad biked around Europe all by himself for nine months before he even went to college," he said. "You could have done that, too, if you'd wanted it bad enough."

And it's true: My husband did in fact earn the money to bike his way across Europe at age 19. Alone.

I taught my sons to stand when an adult enters the room. I taught them to look people in the eye and extend a hand when introduced. I taught them to put their napkins in their laps, not to speak with their mouths full, to stand up for children being bullied. What I had not taught them, it suddenly dawned on me, was how it feels to go through the world as a woman, the mental calculations involved in parking a car downtown or riding an elevator at night or taking a walk in the woods.

"It's dangerous for a woman to camp alone," I finally said at the table that night. "There are women who do it, but I'm not that brave."

My children grew up with stories of their father's adventures. They did not grow up with stories of mine. I didn't tell them the story of the 16-year-old family "friend" who babysat while his parents and mine went out to dinner the year I was 11, how he followed me around the apartment, tugging on my blouse and telling me I should take it off, pulling at the elastic waistband of my pants and telling me I should take them off, how I finally locked myself in my bedroom and didn't come out till my parents got home.

I didn't tell my children the story of walking with my friend to the town hardware store when we were 14. I didn't tell them that my friend used her babysitting money to buy a screwdriver and a deadbolt lock to keep her older brother out of her room at night.

I didn't tell my children the story of my first job, the job I started the week I turned 16, and how the manager kept making excuses to go back to the storeroom whenever I was at the fry station, how he would squeeze his corpulent frame between the counter and me, dragging his sweaty crotch across my rear end on each trip.

I didn't tell my children about the time in graduate school when I had to call the police because there was a man crouching in the bushes next to my front steps, or about the former professor who told me that my impending marriage put an end to the "longest-running act of foreplay" he had ever engaged in. What I had thought of as an avuncular interest in my career he had thought of as an unrealized act of seduction.

There is nothing unusual about these stories. They are the ho-hum, everyday experiences of virtually every woman I know, and such stories rarely get told. There will never be a powerful social-media movement that begins, "Today I ate breakfast" or "Today my dog pooped and I cleaned it up" or "Today I washed my hair with the same shampoo I've been buying since 2006." We tell the stories that are remarkable in some way, stories that are surprising, utterly unexpected. The quotidian doesn't make for a good tale.

And maybe that's why the avalanche of stories on Twitter and Facebook this week has been so powerful. It started on Oct. 5, when The New York Times first broke the story of accusations of sexual harassment against the Hollywood producer Harvey Weinstein, but it became a juggernaut 10 days later, when the actress Alyssa Milano tweeted, "If you've been sexually harassed or assaulted write 'me too' as a reply to this tweet." Within minutes the hashtag #MeToo was all over Twitter, Facebook and Instagram — over 500,000 times on Twitter and 12 million times on Facebook in the first 24 hours alone — and the deluge shows no sign of slowing. The numbers keep ticking up as women tell the stories of men who used their power to overwhelm or coerce them.

I don't know any woman who is surprised by these stories, or by the sheer, vast numbers of them. But men are. Some — by one account 300,000 of them — are writing to point out that they have been harassed, too, because of course the abuse of power isn't gender- or orientation-specific. Others have started their own hashtag: #IHearYou. These are men, like my sons, who have not consistently heard these stories before because for too long women have not considered them stories worth telling. Or because too often such stories are not believed.

It's an irony worth pointing out that the novel I was telling my children about at dinner that night was "Room" by Emma Donoghue, the story of a woman who was kidnapped from her college campus and kept as a sex slave in a backyard shed. Even reading that beautiful, heartbreaking book, it had not occurred to me to tell my children the story of all the times I wanted to go camping or hiking or traveling myself but didn't dare because I couldn't find anyone to go with me.

We have bigger things in this country to worry about than whether producers in Hollywood are sexual predators, and the #MeToo movement is bound to fade again into the background, the way it did after the Bill Cosby allegations came to national prominence, the way it did after accusations against Roger Ailes and Bill O'Reilly. In fact, the first Me Too movement was begun 10 years ago by the African-American activist Tarana Burke, and yet here we are again.

This kind of activism inevitably moves out of the news cycle when the possibility of thermonuclear war becomes a more pressing concern, when global warming becomes a more pressing concern, when desperate refugees in mortal danger become a more pressing concern, when women's ability to make decisions about their own bodies becomes a more pressing concern, when millions of uninsured Americans become a more pressing concern. The list of urgent dangers we now face goes on and on and on. But it's worth noting that most of them can be directly attributed to a man who boasted of being able to violate women at will, and face no consequences at all.

The Woman Who Created #MeToo Long Before Hashtags

BY SANDRA E. GARCIA | OCT. 20, 2017

IN 1997, TARANA BURKE sat across from a 13-year-old girl who had been sexually abused. The young girl was explaining her experience, and it left Ms. Burke speechless. That moment is where the Me Too campaign was born.

"I didn't have a response or a way to help her in that moment, and I couldn't even say 'me too,'" Ms. Burke said.

"It really bothered me, and it sat in my spirit for a long time," she added.

Ten years after that conversation, Ms. Burke created Just Be Inc., a nonprofit organization that helps victims of sexual harassment and assault. She sought out the resources that she had not found readily available to her 10 years before and committed herself to being there for people who had been abused.

And she gave her movement a name: Me Too.

On Sunday, those two words burst into the spotlight of social media with #metoo, a hashtag promoted by the actress Alyssa Milano. Amid the firestorm that ignited, some women of color noted pointedly that the longtime effort by Ms. Burke, who is black, had not received support over the years from prominent white feminists.

Ms. Milano was seeking to give a voice to sexual abuse victims, after accusations of sexual harassment and assault were leveled against the Hollywood producer Harvey Weinstein.

After her tweet, social media was soon flooded with stories of harassment and assault, as #metoo became a way for users to tell their experience with sexual violence and stand in solidarity with other survivors. The hashtag was widely used on Twitter, Facebook, Snapchat and other platforms; on Facebook, it was shared in more than 12 million posts and reactions in the first 24 hours, according to The Associated Press.

It was a particularly combustible moment for social media activism. Days earlier, amid the allegations against Mr. Weinstein, the actress Rose McGowan, who is among those accusing him of sexual harassment, was briefly locked out from her Twitter account, where she had been vocally speaking out against sexual harassment in Hollywood.

The following day, women online participated in a daylong boycott of Twitter, organized around the hashtag #WomenBoycottTwitter. Ms. Milano joined the boycott.

But black, Latino and other women of color started their own campaign. April Reign, a digital media strategist and the woman behind the #OscarSoWhite hashtag, began to organize people around the #WOCAffirmation or women of color affirmation.

The purpose was to uplift one another as they saw a disparity in how women of color were treated when they reported abuse.

"White women have not been as supportive as they could have been of women of color when they experience targeted abuse and harassment," Ms. Reign said in an interview.

"We saw that with Jemele Hill," she said, referring to the sports journalist who was suspended by ESPN this month for speaking out against the N.F.L., "and Leslie Jones," the comedian who was harassed on Twitter last year after being cast in the all-female "Ghostbusters" remake.

"We used it as a peaceful moment to say feminism should be intersectional," Ms. Reign said. "If there is support for Rose McGowan, which is great, you need to be consistent across the board. All women stand with all women."

And so, when Ms. Milano tweeted out the #metoo hashtag without crediting Ms. Burke, some noted that black women had again been left out of the story.

"Women of color are demanded to be silent and are erased," Ms. Reign said. "Like with Tarana."

Ms. Burke, too, said she was alarmed when she saw Ms. Milano's tweet.

"Initially I panicked," she said. "I felt a sense of dread, because something that was part of my life's work was going to be co-opted and taken from me and used for a purpose that I hadn't originally intended."

But Ms. Milano, who said she had been unaware of Ms. Burke's campaign, moved to correct the problem.

She reached out to Ms. Burke two days after she sent out the #metoo tweet and is hoping to collaborate.

"She has been very grateful and gracious," Ms. Burke said.

On Thursday, Ms. Milano went on "Good Morning America," where she publicly credited Ms. Burke for her Me Too campaign.

"What the Me Too campaign really does, and what Tarana Burke has really enabled us to do, is put the focus back on the victims," Ms. Milano said in an interview with Robin Roberts.

Amplifying the voice of the victims has always been Ms. Burke's goal. Despite "a great lack of intersectionality across these various movements," Ms. Burke, whose campaign predates the widespread adoption of social media, said she also believes that the Me Too campaign is bigger than just one person.

"I think it is selfish for me to try to frame Me Too as something that I own," she said. "It is bigger than me and bigger than Alyssa Milano. Neither one of us should be centered in this work. This is about survivors."

The 'Click' Moment: How the Weinstein Scandal Unleashed a Tsunami

BY JESSICA BENNETT | NOV. 5, 2017

IN 1991, WOMEN WORE "I Believe Anita" buttons. Now they post #metoo. Social media, famous accusers and generational change add up to a profound shift.

Forty years ago this month, Ms. magazine put sexual harassment on its cover for the first time. Understanding the sensitivity of the topic, the editors used puppets for the cover image — a male hand reaching into a woman's blouse — rather than a photograph. It was banned from some supermarkets nonetheless.

In 1977, the term sexual harassment had not been defined in the law and had barely entered the public lexicon. And yet, to read that Ms. article today, amid a profound shift in discourse, is to feel haunted by its familiarity.

It describes an executive assistant who quit after her boss asked for oral sex; a student who dropped out after being assaulted by her adviser; a black medical administrator whose white supervisor asked if the women in her neighborhood were prostitutes — and, subsequently, if she would have group sex with him and several colleagues.

Citing a survey in which 88 percent of women said they were harassed at work, the author said the problem permeated almost every profession, but was particularly pernicious "in the supposedly glamorous profession of acting," in which Hollywood's casting couch remained a "strong convention."

"What we have so far seen," the article stated, "is only the tip of a very large and very destructive iceberg."

Four decades later, as allegations against Harvey Weinstein and others continue to metastasize, it feels as if we have crashed into the iceberg. Disaster metaphors — tsunami, hurricane, avalanche, landslide — seem to be in endless rotation to describe the moment, but the point is that a great many powerful men have seen their careers disintegrate, and with astonishing speed.

A great many women — and some men, too — have also spoken out more openly and more forcefully than ever before about what happens behind closed doors or even in the open spaces of studios, newsrooms and other workplaces. Companies have rushed to reassert zero-tolerance policies and whipped together training programs.

We have seen this movie before. Sexual harassment complaints to the United States Equal Employment Opportunity Commission increased 73 percent in the year after Anita Hill's televised testimony about Clarence Thomas's behavior in 1991. Still, Mr. Thomas was confirmed to the Supreme Court, while Ms. Hill went quietly back to being a law professor in Oklahoma. In the ensuing years, the issue cycled between headlines and whispers in a seemingly endless loop.

But this sequel seems to have a surprise ending, or at least a plot twist: The public outrage is deeper and more sustained, and the dominoes continue to fall.

Maybe it's that the accusers this time were famous, media-savvy and mostly white actors with more star power than the accused (unlike, say, Paula Jones vs. Bill Clinton). Maybe it's reflective of a specific period in American history, in which working women of a new generation — those who had grown up with working mothers — decided that enough was enough.

Certainly the endlessly expanding power of social media plays a role: The #metoo hashtag has been used in millions of posts over the past few weeks; been translated into Italian (#QuellaVoltaChe, or "that time when") and French (#BalanceTonPorc, or "out your pig"); and inspired a congressional spinoff.

Several experts likened it to a dam breaking, the cumulative effect of harassment claims over decades and especially the last few years. Some see it as the other shoe dropping after Donald J. Trump's taped boasting about offensive behavior did not block his path to the presidency: He may have gotten away with it, but women were no longer going to let that boss, that mentor, that colleague get away with it, too.

"There is no doubt that having an accused sexual predator in the White House is hanging over this," said Jaclyn Friedman, the author of "Unscrewed: Women, Sex, Power, and How to Stop Letting the System Screw Us All," scheduled for publication this month. "People feel like they can't do anything about that right now, but at least they can do something about this."

AN ARMY OF VOICES

If you are a woman, or know somebody who is, it's safe to assume you have talked about Mr. Weinstein at the dinner table, on the subway, in bed, at work, and any other place where people gather. Perhaps you've asked your partner, your mother, your boss or your friend for the first time, as I have, if she, too, is among this strange new tribe. ("Who was your Weinstein?" we all suddenly want to know.)

I've heard from women who said they've retroactively confronted their harassers and those who enabled them, and from men who are re-examining, perhaps somewhat nervously, their own behavior. The new conversation goes way beyond the workplace to sweep in street harassment, rape culture and "toxic masculinity" — terminology that would have been confined to gender studies classes, not found in mainstream newspapers, not so long ago.

"In the women's movement of the 1970s we had this phrase 'the click moment,'" Barbara Berg, a historian and the author of the 2009 book "Sexism in America: Alive, Well and Ruining Our Future," said. "This is the click moment. It's like, 'Enough.' And then there's a snowball effect: Once you see women speaking truth to power and not being told, 'This is just what you have to put up with,' then it encourages other women to stand up."

With Mr. Weinstein, the accusers were on the record, poised, and more of them seem to emerge each day, so no individual had to bear the burden alone, as Professor Hill had. "When you have Angelina Jolie and Gwyneth Paltrow in the same sentence, well, people take note," the sociologist Michael Kimmel said.

But behind these famous faces was an army of ordinary voices, too, using social media to collectively tell their stories — but also for action. In the case of Bill O'Reilly, remember, it was a coordinated effort, by groups that included the organizers of the Women's March, that urged advertisers to #DropOReilly. They, and Fox News, ultimately did.

Another significant new element is the presence of what many have called silent co-conspirators: dozens of people, over dozens of years, who knew what was going on but did nothing.

"There is this web of enablers," Professor Kimmel, who runs the Center for the Study of Men and Masculinities at Stony Brook University, said. "Bob Weinstein doesn't say to Harvey, 'You better stop or I'll kick you out of the company.' Billy Bush does not say to Donald Trump, 'That's disgusting, not to mention illegal.' In the sexual assault world we often talk about how we incorrectly interpret women's silence as consent. Well, we also mistake men's silence for assent."

A LOOK BACK

If this is a moment of historical social change, it is worth looking at what led us here.

It was two years after that Ms. magazine cover, in 1979, that Catharine A. MacKinnon published a groundbreaking legal argument: that sexual harassment was a form of discrimination under Title VII of the Civil Rights Act of 1964. It was based on a legal theory she had developed while in law school.

That legal argument was tested with Mechelle Vinson, one of a number of African-American women who were involved in early sexual harassment lawsuits — this one a bank teller who said she was repeatedly raped by her married boss. In 1986, her case, with Professor MacKinnon's help, was part of a Supreme Court ruling that enshrined the harassment-as-discrimination theory into law.

Then came Professor Hill, whose televised testimony about Mr. Thomas, her former boss — at the E.E.O.C., of all places — was, Ms. Berg said, in effect "home-schooling a generation of Americans in what sexual harassment was." Almost immediately, the phone hotline for 9to5, a support group for working women, began ringing off the hook.

"People were almost bewildered," the group's director told The New York Times in 1992. "You mean this is sexual harassment? You mean I could do something about this?"

Ms. Berg said she remembers a former colleague calling to ask, of their former boss, "Did he proposition you, too?" (He had.) Professor Kimmel said his mother told him over dinner that she was harassed in graduate school.

"It was literally water-cooler conversation everywhere," said Freada Kapor Klein, who conducted one of the first surveys on sexual harassment in the 1970s.

But most of those stories were shared in private — in part because of what the world watched Professor Hill endure. Before an all-male Senate judiciary panel, she was accused of bringing "sleaze" into the nomination process, portrayed as suffering from delusional fantasies, and famously called, by the pundit David Brock, "a little bit nutty and a little bit slutty."

"I remember the anger of that moment," Teresa Younger, then a 22-year-old nanny and now president of the Ms. Foundation for Women, said. "Anita Hill was the example of a strong, accomplished black woman, and if she of all people could be discredited then it seemed women, particularly women of color, had no voice when it came to sexual harassment."

FROM 'I BELIEVE' TO #METOO

It's worth noting that the campaign slogan back then, on buttons and bumper stickers rather than Facebook and Twitter, was not "Me Too" but "I Believe Anita" — a message of solidarity, not self-exposure.

After Professor Hill came Ms. Jones, whose lawsuit against Mr. Clinton was dismissed. Others won in court but struggled in the aftermath: Paula Coughlin, a Navy lieutenant who was sexually assaulted by drunken officers, was sidelined and ultimately quit her job. Rena Weeks, a law secretary who was harassed by a partner, never worked again.

"I think for a long time it shut women up, at least publicly," Professor Kimmel said.

In her 2017 book, "Butterfly Politics," Professor MacKinnon adapts a concept from chaos theory in which the tiny motion of a butterfly's wings can trigger a tornado half a world away. Under the right conditions, she posits, small actions can produce major social transformations.

"Ashley Judd is the butterfly of this moment," Professor MacKinnon said of the actor who began the recent groundswell of accusations against Mr. Weinstein. "She is the one who broke it open, who has made this possible for so many other women. And so you have an explosion of it because it's for so long been suppressed."

Professor Kimmel, the sociologist, said, "There comes a tipping point when the 'frame' changes." "One day, segregated water fountains seemed 'normal' if you were a white Southerner," he noted. "It's just how things were. Then they're illegal, and a few years later you say, 'Wow, how did we ever see that as O.K.?'"

Ms. Friedman, though, said she is waiting for an important moment: "When are we going to start believing people the first time?"

"When is it going to be that one instance is enough, and that you don't have to find out 30 years later?" she asked. "I also worry that there is the possibility for this to be treated like a cancer, and now Harvey is gone so the cancer is excised. But Harvey is not the only cancer."

'The Silence Breakers' Named Time's Person of the Year for 2017

BY JONAH ENGEL BROMWICH | DEC. 6, 2017

FIRST IT WAS A STORY. Then a moment. Now, two months after women began to come forward in droves to accuse powerful men of sexual harassment and assault, it is a movement.

Time magazine has named "the silence breakers" its person of the year for 2017, referring to those women, and the global conversation they have started.

The magazine's editor in chief, Edward Felsenthal, said in an interview on the "Today" show on Wednesday that the #MeToo movement represented the "fastest-moving social change we've seen in decades, and it began with individual acts of courage by women and some men too."

Investigations published in October by The New York Times and The New Yorker, both of them detailing multiple allegations of sexual harassment and assault against the movie producer Harvey Weinstein, sparked the sudden rush of women coming forward.

In a joint interview after the choice was announced, Tarana Burke, who created the Me Too mantra years ago, and the actress Alyssa Milano, who helped promote it more recently, focused on what was still left to do.

"I've been saying from the beginning that it's not just a moment, it's a movement," Ms. Burke said. "I think now the work really begins. The hashtag is a declaration. But now we're poised to really stand up and do the work."

Ms. Milano agreed, laying out her aspirations for the movement.

"I want companies to take on a code of conduct, I want companies to hire more women, I want to teach our children better," she said. "These are all things that we have to set in motion, and as women we have to support each other and stand together and say that's it, we're done, no more."

It is a testament to the size of the movement that the set of "Today" itself, where the announcement was made, had recently been the site of such a reckoning. Matt Lauer, one of NBC's most well-known personalities for decades, was fired only last week after an allegation of sexual harassment from a subordinate. Other complaints soon followed.

And of course, Time's 2017 runner-up for person of the year, Donald J. Trump, was accused during his presidential campaign by more than 10 women of sexual misconduct, from unwanted touching to sexual assault.

Those accusations did not stop Mr. Trump from being named person of the year in 2016. And Mr. Trump inadvertently promoted this year's announcement, tweeting that he had been told he would "probably" be chosen again and claiming to have turned down the honor. Time quickly released a statement saying that the president was incorrect.

Time has been using the title for more than nine decades to drum up interest in one of its tentpole issues. The magazine chose its first group, as opposed to a single "man of the year" (and back then it was a man), in 1950, when it selected "the American Fighting-man." The title was changed to the neutral "person of the year" in 1999.

Other groups have included "Americans under 25" in 1966, "The Whistleblowers" in 2002 and, memorably, "You" in 2006.

In 1975, the magazine chose "American women," profiling a dozen who it said "symbolized the new consciousness of women generally." It would be a decade before Time selected another woman.

CHAPTER 2

The International Response to #MeToo

Within days of its appearance on social media, the #MeToo movement spread internationally. Women from France created their own hashtag through which they shared stories of sexual harassment and offered support. Swedish women pointed out by the thousands the hypocrisy of living in a feminist country and yet still being subjected to sexual assault and harassment. Italian women largely ignored #MeToo on the assumption that nothing would change given Italy's deeply patriarchal society. The Canadian government began to develop bills to reform sexual harassment laws.

France Considers Fines for Catcalls as Women Speak Out on Harassment

BY DAN BILEFSKY AND ELIAN PELTIER | OCT. 17, 2017

ON FRIDAY AFTERNOON, the journalist Sandra Muller turned to Twitter to recall a humiliating and inappropriate sexual come-on from a powerful French executive.

"You have big breasts. You are my type of woman. I will make you orgasm all night," she quoted him as having said, adding the hashtag #BalanceTonPorc, or "Expose Your Pig."

By Tuesday, tens of thousands of Frenchwomen had heeded that call, posting disturbing accounts of sexual harassment and abuse, although most stopped short of identifying their harassers.

This response to the scandal engulfing the Hollywood producer Harvey Weinstein was akin to the Twitter outpouring in the United States and elsewhere under the hashtag #MeToo, inspired in part by a tweet from the actress Alyssa Milano. In France, however, where a chauvinistic culture has long enabled powerful men to misbehave with impunity, the social media debate may push forward changes not only in the culture but in the law.

Proposals are under discussion to fine men for aggressive catcalling or lecherous behavior toward women in public, to extend the statute of limitations in cases of sexual assault involving minors, and to create a new age ceiling under which minors cannot legally consent to a sexual relationship.

Marlène Schiappa, a feminist and writer who is France's junior minister for gender equality, said on Monday that the government was considering precisely how to define street harassment and how much to fine. The government would consult legal professionals on its proposals and hold workshops for citizens across the country, she said, aiming to put measures before Parliament next year.

Speaking to RTL radio, Ms. Schiappa said she had been deeply struck by the response to the #BalanceTonPorc hashtag.

"We all have stories of harassment and assault," she said, adding: "One of my best friends said something with this hashtag that she had never told our group of friends. This hashtag, with the barrier created by a screen, can help people speak out, and I think that it is truly beneficial."

Some commentators argued that sexual harassment accusations would be better handled in a courtroom than on social media. "Denouncing sexual harassment on a social network with a hashtag isn't the appropriate place at all," said Christophe Noël, a labor lawyer. "It can rebound on the accuser and create an open door to excesses and defamation."

Ms. Muller, the journalist who first tweeted the "Expose Your Pig" hashtag, said in a phone interview on Tuesday that although she was overwhelmed by the hundreds of reactions she had received, she didn't want Twitter to become a tribunal. "I'm not a judge," she said.

Two lawyers for the executive Ms. Muller named in her tweet demanded on Tuesday that she delete it; one of the lawyers, Nicolas Bénoit, called her accusation a case of defamation but declined to comment further. The executive didn't respond to requests for an interview.

In France, the Weinstein affair has recalled the case of Dominique Strauss-Kahn, the former International Monetary Fund chief and one-time presidential contender who was arrested in New York in 2011 and accused of assaulting a hotel housekeeper. Those charges were dropped, but helped dent a longstanding French reluctance to breach the privacy of public figures, no matter their sexual transgressions. Sandrine Rousseau, a former leader of the French Green Party and leading advocate for victims of sexual harassment, said the Weinstein case had particular resonance in France because women had suffered in silence for so long.

Ms. Rousseau was one of a dozen women who in 2016 accused a Green Party legislator, Denis Baupin, of sexual harassment, saying he had pushed her up against a wall and kissed her against her will. Mr. Baupin, who resigned as vice president of France's National Assembly, denied the accusations and the case was dropped on the grounds that too much time had elapsed.

"DSK was the first blow, and Baupin the second one," Ms. Rousseau said in an interview, referring to the initials of Dominique Strauss-Kahn. "The Weinstein revelations have had a strong echo in France, because what used to be seen as naughtiness is now being considered as sexual harassment."

Ms. Rousseau said "Expose Your Pig" was a good start, but words needed to be translated into action and successful legal cases remained rare. According to a 2016 study by Ifop, a leading pollster, just 65 of the 1,048 sexual harassment lawsuits in France in 2014 led to a conviction.

But the atmosphere may be changing. In December, Georges Tron, who was a mayor and a government official under former President Nicolas Sarkozy, will stand trial on accusations of rape and sexual harassment after two women said he had assaulted them in a locked room in the town hall when he was mayor of Draveil, south of Paris. Mr. Tron resigned in 2011 over the accusations, which he denies.

In Europe, several countries have moved in recent years to criminalize sexual harassment, including Portugal, where the left-leaning government in 2015 made verbal sexual abuse a crime with a fine of up to 120 euros, or about $142. Belgium has also moved against sexual harassment, and in 2014 introduced penalties including a jail sentence of up to one year for remarks intending to express contempt for a person because of his or her gender.

In a sign of how French mores have evolved, President Emanuel Macron on Sunday announced that he had begun the procedure to strip Mr. Weinstein of France's highest award, the Legion of Honor, which he had received in 2012 for his work promoting foreign cinema in the United States.

Brigitte Macron, the French first lady, has congratulated victims of sexual harassment or violence for sharing their stories, and she expressed hope that something positive could come out of the "bad" of the Weinstein affair.

Several French actresses are among the more than two dozen women who have stepped forward with accusations against Mr. Weinstein, among them Florence Darel, Judith Godrèche and Léa Seydoux, who starred in the James Bond film "Spectre."

Ms. Seydoux wrote in The Guardian newspaper that when she first encountered Mr. Weinstein, he asked her to meet him for a drink and that he invited her to his hotel room.

"It was hard to say no because he's so powerful," she wrote. "We were talking on the sofa when he suddenly jumped on me and tried to kiss me. I had to defend myself. He's big and fat, so I had to be forceful to resist him. I left his room, thoroughly disgusted."

She added: "I wasn't afraid of him, though. Because I knew what kind of man he was all along."

AURELIEN BREEDEN CONTRIBUTED REPORTING.

'Revolt' in France Against Sexual Harassment Hits Cultural Resistance

BY ALISSA J. RUBIN | NOV. 19, 2017

PARIS — In the icy winter of 1905, many of the women who hand-painted the world-famous Limoges vases and figurines went on strike in France — not because they were poorly paid or toiled long hours, but because they were prey to the factory overseer's sexual urges.

Their protest was against the custom, inherited from the Middle Ages, in which bosses (or feudal lords) compelled sexual services from the young women who worked for them.

A different kind of protest against sexual abuse is underway in France and America in the wake of the accusations of abuse by the Hollywood producer Harvey Weinstein. These new protesters are armed with hashtags like #MeToo and #BalanceTonPorc, or "Out Your Pig."

But not everyone is so sure that the current wave of outrage on social media will be enough to change behavior and attitudes that have resisted generations of efforts in France.

"It is not at all the same thing to tweet in 140 characters and to bring a complaint in court," said Marilyn Baldeck, a legal professional who works with the European Association Against Violence Against Women at Work.

Other recent watersheds in France brought little relief for women in their wake. The sexual assault trial that derailed the presidential hopes of Dominique Strauss-Kahn, the former managing director of the International Monetary Fund, crossed a threshold in France for making the private lives of public figures fair game for the news media.

But the sheer number of women in France currently going public with the details of their unwanted sexual encounters makes clear that the private behavior of powerful men — or, for that matter, less-powerful men — did not necessarily change.

Similarly, after a flurry of sexual harassment allegations roiled France's National Assembly last year, some of the laws approved by the same body may have raised the hurdles for women to prosecute harassers.

Lawyers and experts have criticized recent changes in the labor law, ordered by President Emmanuel Macron, for backsliding and say that, at every level, the administration's response has been either nonexistent or inadequate.

Some women in France feel so aggrieved that they started a petition addressed to Mr. Macron, urging him to treat sexual harassment as a national emergency; it gained 100,000 signatures in its first three days online.

"What's happening is a revolt," said Geneviève Fraisse, a French philosopher, writer on feminist thought and director of research at the government's National Center for Scientific Research.

"It's the same thing that happened for abortion in the 1970s and for equal pay in the 1990s," she added. "It's a catalyst. It's not something that can be ignored; it's an historic moment."

But there remain big obstacles, cultural and legal, that discourage women from complaining about harassment in the workplace. A culture of silence has long persisted around such behavior, and is only now being broken.

France's reluctance to move more aggressively against sexual harassment reflects deeply rooted ideas about sexual relations and the relative power between men and women, said Joan Scott, a professor emeritus of intellectual and cultural history at the Institute for Advanced Study in Princeton, N.J., who has studied French social and sexual mores.

"There is a longstanding commitment to the notion that the French do gender relations differently — especially from prudish Americans — and that has to do with the French understanding of seduction," she said. "Seduction is the alternative to thinking about it as sexual harassment."

Christine Bard, a professor of feminism at the University of Angers, echoed those thoughts. There is an "idealization of seduction 'à la Française,' and that anti-feminism has become almost part of the national identity and is seen as a retort to Anglo-American culture," she said.

"The desire to distance ourselves from a 'puritanism' which is 'Protestant,' 'Anglo-Saxon' and 'feminist' plays well notably in intellectual milieus, and anti-Americanism has been a constant dimension of anti-feminism in France for more than a century," Ms. Bard said.

Sexual harassment in the workplace was made subject to legal sanction in France starting only in 1992, in the wake of Anita Hill's accusations during the confirmation hearings of Clarence Thomas, then a Supreme Court nominee.

DMITRY KOSTYUKOV FOR THE NEW YORK TIMES

Karima Emtir, left, and Houria Dahmani at the Gare du Nord in Paris on Nov. 10. They and two other colleagues sued their employer, H. Reinier, a subcontractor to France's national rail company, which had not fired a team manager they accused of harassment. They won a modest settlement.

That controversy riveted France, which created, at about the same time, a civil and a criminal offense of sexual harassment. But the reach of those laws was not matched by vigorous enforcement, labor lawyers say. The effect has been to discourage women from pursuing cases, as reflected in a 2014 survey for France's Defender of Rights, a government office that helps people enforce their civil rights.

The survey found that at least one in five working women said they had confronted sexual harassment. But only 30 percent of them had reported it to management, and only 5 percent ever brought it before a judge. Far more said they had worked in an environment where there were sexist or crude jokes.

Ms. Baldeck, the legal professional, notes that many women do not pursue claims "because it is too difficult since the judiciary is so poorly equipped to deal with these complaints."

"In France, 93 percent of complaints of criminal sexual harassment are not followed up on" because of insufficient staffing and funding, she said.

There is no French equivalent of the Equal Employment Opportunity Commission in the United States, which can bring cases but which also works directly with companies to resolve them through internal measures before they go to court.

Moreover, in 40 percent of French harassment cases, the person who complained was punished by management rather than the accused. Some women were blocked as they tried to seek higher positions, while others did not have their contracts renewed or were fired.

While many of the men recently accused of offenses in the United States and Britain have been forced to resign, in France, it remains the norm in both the public and private sectors for those accused of offenses to stay in their jobs.

That puts victims in a difficult situation and can mean that their harassment may continue or even worsen once a complaint is made. The situation has been particularly tough for women trying to break into traditionally male jobs in the French government bureaucracy.

The government's internal administrative tribunal is deliberating the case of a 35-year-old who in 2009 became one of the first women to be admitted to an elite branch of the police.

One of two women assigned to a division of 150 special police officers, she charges that she was quickly ostracized and made the target of repeated sexual jokes.

It started with the men insisting that they kiss the policewomen hello on both cheeks; she wanted to shake hands. When she insisted, some of the men refused to do so.

One of her colleagues made masturbating gestures in front of her to insult her, and one called her a "dirty whore," she said. After she was injured while on a mission, she did not return to her job.

In defense of her colleagues, the Ministry of Interior countered that "smutty jokes" were to be expected in a force where people worked closely together and de facto "lacked privacy and where the work culture is exclusively masculine."

It added that the missions were difficult and that some male police officers had not "entirely assimilated" a new code of conduct with the introduction of women.

But, still, what she had experienced did not rise to the level of sexual harassment, the ministry said in a written statement.

In a different case, even after four female cleaners sued their employer, H. Reinier, a subcontractor working for France's national rail company, their harasser kept his job while one of the women was fired.

But such obstacles are not new. The female pottery painters who protested their mistreatment at the Limoges porcelain factories in 1905 won their fight only after the strikes turned violent and the army opened fire, killing one man and wounding four others.

The local news media at the time described a funeral procession of as many as 30,000 workers, "many of them women, who carried flowers in their hands as a last homage to someone who had died fighting for their dignity."

ELIAN PELTIER CONTRIBUTED REPORTING FROM PARIS.

A #MeToo Moment
for the European Parliament

BY MILAN SCHREUER | OCT. 25, 2017

BRUSSELS — The #MeToo movement reached the European Parliament on Wednesday, when several members spoke about their experiences with sexual harassment during a debate over ways to combat the abuse of women.

"Me too," said Terry Reintke, 30, a German member of the European Parliament for the Greens. "I have been sexually harassed, just like millions of other people in the European Union."

The open discussion of sexual harassment spread to Europe last week, after the torrent of allegations against Harvey Weinstein, the Hollywood producer, the television host Bill O'Reilly and others.

The session in Strasbourg, France, lasted for only 90 minutes and had been hastily scheduled after European news outlets published a series of anonymous reports about sexual harassment allegations against members of the Parliament and in the European Union's offices in Brussels. About 45 female and five male members spoke for one to two minutes each to a mostly empty auditorium.

"At least one in every three women has been victim of some sort of physical or sexual violence," Cecilia Malmstrom, the European commissioner for trade, said during the session. "But these statistics do not tell enough personal stories, and the reason we are debating this today is of course because of the global movement of #MeToo."

Several lawmakers called for the ratification of the Istanbul Convention, which would require member states to adopt a comprehensive legal framework to combat violence against women. As of today, the convention has been ratified by only 15 of the European Union's 28 member states.

Several of the lawmakers also called for the adoption of a resolution put forward during the debate on combating sexual harassment. The measure will be voted on on Thursday.

Ms. Reintke demanded measures to "improve the mechanisms for fighting sexual harassment" in the European Parliament after the "shocking reports about the events" there.

Harassment has also been reported to be widespread throughout the European Union bureaucracy in Brussels, especially among junior assistants, interns and trainees. Such assistants usually have precarious work contracts, making them particularly vulnerable.

Grainne Hutton, 24, a former intern from Leeds, England, is one of dozens of women who decided to speak out over the past week about sexual harassment in the "Brussels bubble."

After earning a degree in international affairs, Ms. Hutton said in an email, she was thrilled to land a six-month internship in Brussels at "one of the top consultancies."

But in the course of her internship, she said, her supervisor began to behave in ways that made her increasingly uncomfortable.

"Lewd sexual comments were made in meetings, over the company messenger and over Facebook," she said. "He would message me after midnight, extremely crude and disgustingly sexual things. He would also use our internal messaging channels to send me messages about his favorite animals having sex, asking me about my sex life and other perturbing and intrusive questions. He would even say things in internal meetings in front of others. This went on for over a month."

Ms. Hutton put up with her boss, she said, because she was worried about missing out on a possible job offer and then not finding work elsewhere. But when he did offer to hire her at the end of her internship, she declined.

"I have suffered from sexual harassment, but this does not define me," she said. "Brussels was and will always be one of my favorite places in the world. This being said, there is a systemic problem of sexual harassment within the Brussels bubble."

Yes, It Happens in Sweden, #Too

BY JENNY NORDBERG | DEC. 15, 2017

CISSI WALLIN was sitting in a TriBeCa diner this October when she first saw the story on Harvey Weinstein's alleged sexual assaults and harassment of women. An actor and writer based in Stockholm, the 32-year-old Ms. Wallin had come to Manhattan on vacation with her husband and toddler son, and as she kept on reading, she silently asked herself: "What if people would believe me now?"

Ms. Wallin had filed a police report in 2011, a few years after she was sexually assaulted, only to see it dismissed within weeks. Now she decided to do something different: She put the name of a well-known columnist for Sweden's largest left-wing tabloid newspaper on her Instagram page, alongside a statement saying he had drugged and violently raped her in Stockholm more than a decade ago.

Soon more people came forward about the man. I was a co-author of an investigation into his behavior.

And suddenly, just as in the United States, stories of other national figures in the arts and media began pouring forth. About men who had used their professional power and influence to harass or abuse younger, often subordinate women, often at work. About situations in which "everyone knew," but men viewed as indispensable had been protected by management for years (sometimes the perpetrators were management). In contrast to the situation in the United States, however, the wave quickly grew beyond accusations against the famous and powerful: Tens of thousands of Swedish women have signed a series of appeals in the national press detailing incidents of brutal sexual assault and harassment in almost every professional field, from law, medicine and academia to politics and defense. Committed by Swedish men.

So yes, it happens in Sweden, #too.

This reckoning in a country that sees itself as best in class on gender equality has been particularly painful. With a feminist government, a feminist foreign policy, a national agency tasked with upholding all things equality and a prime minister who calls himself a feminist, shouldn't we be better than this? Shouldn't these impossibly perfect-looking, tall men who go on government-paid paternal leave be a little, well, more evolved by now?

Or not.

As someone who has lived and worked in both Sweden and the United States, I've seen sexual harassment in both places over decades. In my experience, the American workplace is more openly sexualized and flirtatious, a place where women are expected to be open and enthusiastic to advances by men, whether in the form of offers of mentorship that must happen over dinner or as more direct abuses of power.

Sweden, on the other hand, is more cold, correct and asexual on the surface. But give a Swedish man a drink or two after work, and you'll be surprised how quickly many of them will take out their various frustrations in the form of lewd behavior against women, only to seamlessly go back to voicing egalitarian ideals the next day. As an acquaintance who immigrated to Stockholm from Britain once observed, "Sweden is a progressive, but not a sophisticated, society."

How well can reams of pro-gender equality rules and regulations really protect women in this cultural context? According to those who study such things, not very. Sweden is an open society but one that retains "traditional sexual norms," said Madeleine Leijonhufvud, a criminal law professor who is retired from Stockholm University. Women work alongside men and move freely in society, but ultimately, it's still always viewed as a woman's responsibility to protect herself from men. In that sense, women are not yet fully protected by the justice system: Very few rape charges even lead to a trial, and Ms. Leijonhufvud says that when they do, "a woman's circumstances and appearance are always questioned — only in this type of crime is there a peculiar presumption that victims of crime will lie."

Sweden is also not a place where pretty much anyone gets fired. Ever. A full-time staff job is perceived as a right, and the employer's responsibility to handle and protect a problematic employee will often supersede the concern for a safe workplace environment for women. So most men accused of sexual harassment or even rape in Sweden still hold their jobs.

The generous take on why #MeToo has prompted stories from women across Swedish society is that its women are brave and empowered enough to rally, albeit largely anonymously. (As perhaps befits a culture that focuses on the collective rather than the individual, most of the stories in Sweden have left both accused and accuser unnamed.) The more depressing thought may be that in a society where there is a law, a fine-tuned rule and a government agency for each aspect of life, pervasive abuse may be more effectively denied or trivialized for longer. We find ourselves incredulous that such things could happen here, despite all of our (very expensive) efforts at becoming the world's best place to live.

Because who can really stand that in the place where a little girl has the best chance of being born with everything — a free education, health care and a social welfare cushion to fall back on — when she attempts to do meaningful work, there's still no escaping from the pervasive law of male supremacy?

In some ways, perhaps it has been less painful for all of us to join the silence about our own professional lives, instead moving on to what we imagined were bigger, better things, things that contributed to "the greater good." When feminism morphs into a collective consensus and an abstract truth, rather than an individual act of struggle and personal responsibility, maybe we fail to be brave.

Victims of anything is not who we want to be, and certainly not how we, the free and unbroken pioneers of gender equality, can bear to see ourselves. It also makes our shame deeper now — because to how many younger colleagues have we coldly and pragmatically hinted that this too shall pass?

The really desperate thought is that if this is Sweden, where is the rest of the world?

While we all ponder that notion, Sweden's diplomats and foreign aid workers will continue to deliver lectures on gender equality to other countries. We're experts at that. And The New York Times, along with other publications, will continue to report on curious and beautiful Swedish customs and traditions, to entice readers with the fantasy of a country that seems to have gotten almost everything right, in both aesthetics and quality of life.

Call it the Swedish way.

In Italy, #MeToo Is More Like 'Meh'

BY JASON HOROWITZ | DEC. 16, 2017

ROME — The women took their seats behind each of the more than 600 desks in Italy's lower house of Parliament and listened to Laura Boldrini, the chamber's president, talk about how the "Weinstein scandal" had set off a worldwide reckoning with sexual harassment and misconduct.

With one notable exception, that is.

"In Italy, it certainly hasn't had the same effect. In our country, there are no harassers," Ms. Boldrini said sarcastically, drawing chuckles throughout the hall.

In truth, Ms. Boldrini said, harassment was rife, but Italian women feared the repercussions of speaking up: "They know that in this country, there is a strong prejudice against them."

By turning Montecitorio Palace into a women-only institution on a recent Saturday, Ms. Boldrini hoped to emphasize how sexual harassment and abuse against women are often ignored by what she and many others consider a stubbornly patriarchal society.

Since the revelations about Harvey Weinstein's abuse of women were exposed in October, politicians, actors and powerful media figures have resigned in disgrace in the United States, and women have flooded social media with their own stories of sexual harassment and assault, using the hashtag #MeToo.

In Italy, it's mostly "meh."

"This historic moment doesn't mean much to Italy, sadly," said Asia Argento, an Italian actress whose accusations of sexual harassment against Mr. Weinstein drew signs of solidarity abroad but a good deal of eye-rolling and insults at home. "Nothing has changed."

That apathy extends beyond the Italian entertainment industry. In Florence, defense lawyers for paramilitary police officers accused of raping two young American women sought to ask the accusers if they had been wearing underwear that night. In Sicily, a court cleared a man of sexual harassment charges, determining that sophomoric humor, rather than sexual intent, had motivated his groping of colleagues.

And the former prime minister Silvio Berlusconi is staging a comeback six years after being forced out of power amid mass protests and trials examining his role in so-called Bunga Bunga bacchanals with underage women and prostitutes.

"For us, defending women is a priority and it always has been," Mr. Berlusconi, who was cleared of soliciting underage prostitutes but is still fighting charges that he bribed a witness, said in a recent television interview.

That is not to suggest that the 81-year-old, whose girlfriend is nearly 50 years his junior, has changed his ways. In October, he told a crowd of supporters on the island of Ischia that he had introduced the bidet to Col. Muammar el-Qaddafi and in so doing "taught these lusty Africans that there's also foreplay."

The audience applauded.

"It's not shocking, because in the end, Italians think it's normal," Lorella Zanardo, a women's rights advocate and filmmaker, said of the muted reaction to reports of sexual harassment in the country. Especially in high-profile fields such as film, politics and the media, she said, "the idea of a woman advancing her career by giving or selling her body, it's taken for granted."

Mr. Berlusconi himself has contributed to the country's perception of women as decorative objects of desire, Ms. Zanardo said, by casting them as scantily clad adornments on his television channels. But she acknowledged that the popularity and durability of those shows over the last 40 years showed an eager audience among Italians, many of whom still think of women in archetypes of care-taking madonnas or corrupting Jezebels, with little room in between.

Perhaps nowhere has the view of sex as a transactional feature of Italian life been as stark as in the backlash against Ms. Argento.

The daughter of Italy's most famous director of horror movies, she describes living a nightmare since becoming one of the first women to make a public accusation against Mr. Weinstein, whom she said performed oral sex on her against her will. She says she is afraid to leave her house, and plans to flee the country in response to particularly virulent attacks in the news media.

Alessandro Sallusti, the editor of the conservative daily Il Giornale, said on Italian television in October that Ms. Argento's public accusations decades after the events took place amounted to her being an "accomplice." (As he spoke, the camera slowly panned over the legs of the actress seated next to him.)

Another right-wing paper repeatedly argued that Ms. Argento knowingly entered into a transactional relationship to further her career, and even people whom Ms. Argento might have expected to count among her allies instead cast doubt on her innocence.

In a Twitter post, the transgender Italian actress and former member of Parliament Vladimir Luxuria blamed Ms. Argento for not "saying no" to Weinstein "as other actresses did," and for failing to report the alleged assault at the time. Natalia Aspesi, a self-described feminist, said that Ms. Argento should not have been surprised by how things progressed after she agreed to give Mr. Weinstein a massage.

In response, Ms. Argento has cast herself as the avenging angel of the Italian Twitterverse, promoting the hashtag #quellavoltache, or "the time that," which was conceived as an Italian answer to #metoo but has had far less impact. Her avatar depicts her raising a fist, and her account bio reads, "I was born for such a time as this #noshamefist."

She has accused an unidentified Italian actor-director of exposing himself to her when she was 16, and a "Hollywood big shot director" with drugging and raping her when she was 26. She warns that abused women know where sexual predators sleep, has resurfaced accusations in tabloids and maligned the "misogynistic patriarchal Italian society" where "sex assault victims are shamed."

Ms. Zanardo, the rights advocate and filmmaker, said that to institute cultural change would require teaching Italian children to respect women as equals.

The #MeToo Moment:
What Happened After Women
Broke the Silence Elsewhere?

BY SOMINI SENGUPTA | DEC. 22, 2017

AMERICA WASN'T FIRST. Women in other countries have broken their silence about sexual misconduct, too, in recent years.

Usually, it was an act of heinous violence that uncorked the rage. Women took to the streets, including in deeply patriarchal societies. Sometimes, they got laws changed. Sometimes that wasn't enough.

India's #MeToo moment came in December 2012, after a 23-year-old woman named Jyoti Singh was gang-raped so viciously that it damaged her intestines, lungs and brain. Along with angry protests, stories spilled out from ordinary Indian women — including many of my friends — about degradation they had been too ashamed to speak of before.

Morocco had a moment in 2012 as well, after the suicide of Amina Filali, a 16-year-old who had been forced to marry a man who raped her at gunpoint. Public outcry forced lawmakers to scrap a law that allowed rapists to be exonerated through marriage.

In 2016, Latin America exploded about what would come to be known as femicide — the killings of women because they are women — and the campaign came with a visceral hashtag: #NiUnaMenos, or in English, "not one less."

Perhaps the outcry against violence against women has been especially intense precisely because violence against women is so pervasive. It is so, infuriatingly, everyday.

Globally, according to the World Health Organization, 35 percent of women experience either physical or sexual violence at the hands of their intimate partner or sexual violence at the hands of someone else.

Sit on that for a second: 35 percent. One in three women.

Underlying that figure is women's silence, as though we had all signed an invisible nondisclosure agreement at birth. Only occasionally, when acts of extreme violence shock us to the core, do we look up and instead of despairing, we speak. We tell our stories to each other. But then what happens?

LAWS GOT CHANGED. BEHAVIOR TAKES LONGER.

In Morocco, two years after Amina Filali's suicide, the law that allowed her accused rapist to evade prosecution by marrying her was revoked. Lebanon and Jordan made similar moves this year.

Feminists in the Arab world celebrated, but cautiously. Changing law was the first step, they told me when I was reporting earlier this year from Lebanon. Changing behavior would be harder.

Women and girls would have to come forward to report rape. Their families would have to defend them, rather than force them to marry their abusers to absolve them of what's regarded as a collective familial shame.

"These are cases that are not discussed in public," is how Maya Ammar, a spokeswoman for Kafa, a group that works with survivors, put it. "They all happen in silence."

Many Latin American countries had already passed a raft of laws against gender violence, including some against femicide, by the time a "harrowing succession" of killings in Argentina unleashed new outrage in 2015.

Protests spread to Peru the next year and, this November, prompted defiance in an unlikely arena: a beauty pageant.

One contestant, instead of announcing her bust and waist measurements, announced how many women had been killed in femicides in 2017 — 2,202, as my colleagues Nicholas Casey and Susan Abad reported.

"One woman spoke of children who die from sexual abuse," the story continued. "Another said 70 percent of women had been victims of attacks on the streets of Peru."

The Association for Women's Rights in Development, an international feminist organization, credited #NiUnaMenos for what it called "tangible change" in several countries.

Legislators in Uruguay, for example, made femicide an aggravating circumstance to murder, potentially stiffening punishment for those convicted. Peru plans to establish a registry of gender violence convicts. And Argentina has been forced to figure out how to implement gender-violence laws long on the books. Gabriela Wiener, a Peruvian writer, was bullish about the-not-so tangible changes, writing in our Opinion section that "from the moment women in Peru named the mistreatment we suffered in our community, as in a spell, we cast evil a bit away, so there would be not one fewer of us."

YEARS PASS. MOMENTUM SLOWS.

India is the country of my birth, and I was in Delhi five years ago when Jyoti Singh was assaulted on her way home from the movies on a cold December night.

She lived long enough to tell the awful story to the police. That emboldened thousands of survivors to file police reports after they had been assaulted. Rape laws were strengthened; police departments promised reform.

I wrote hopefully about this moment in my 2016 book, "The End of Karma: Hope and Fury Among India's Young." Indian women were refusing to stay silent. The country was being forced to listen. This was a moment.

It's hard for me to be hopeful now.

Recently, Human Right Watch published a dispiriting report, detailing how the reforms that were promised (and made in some instances) remain meaningless for many.

Police are reluctant to initiate criminal investigations, particularly if the victim's family is considered to be low on the caste ladder. Medical professionals continue to subject survivors to degrading examinations. Victims are shamed in court.

"The police beat me up, detained my father, and threatened to lock him up under false charges if I didn't tell the magistrate that I had filed a false complaint of rape, so I did as they said," one woman told Human Rights Watch.

It makes me wonder what will come of this #MeToo moment five years from now.

In Canada, a 'Perfect Storm' for a #MeToo Reckoning

BY IAN AUSTEN AND CATHERINE PORTER | JAN. 29, 2018

OTTAWA — Michelle Rempel was debating a sexual harassment bill in Canada's House of Commons on Monday when she suddenly fell silent. Ms. Rempel, a Conservative lawmaker from Alberta, dropped her prepared remarks onto her desk, stretched out her arms and turned her palms up.

"I don't want to sit in this place and have this conversation again," she told the chamber. "I don't want another woman coming into my office. This needs to stop and it needs to stop now."

Monday's frank debate in Canada's seat of power about sexual harassment and politics was the latest, and most potent, response to the #MeToo movement that is sweeping the nation in ways that have surprised even hardened Canadian feminists.

In a country that often defines itself in the ways it is different from its larger and more bellicose American neighbor, Canadian women have been both inspired and dispirited by what is happening across the border and moved to speak out themselves.

One notable difference, however, is that Canadian politicians from all parties are strongly calling for changes and supporting victims who are increasingly coming forward.

"The MeToo and Time's Up movements have helped women and other survivors from around the world to bring their stories forward and shine a spotlight on harassment and sexual violence," said Patty Hajdu, Canada's labor minister, while opening the debate on stronger sexual harassment protection legislation in the House of Commons, "and it's our responsibility to ensure that light does not fade."

One lawmaker after another rose to support her bill, and in some cases, argue that it should be strengthened.

The debate came, coincidentally, as Canada is reeling from a maelstrom of accusations of sexually inappropriate behavior against men in positions of power, and their swift removal.

Just last week, two provincial Conservative Party leaders and a federal cabinet minister resigned. Outside of politics, one of the most prominent members of Toronto's theater community quit the company he founded, accused in a lawsuit of sexual harassment. And last fall, two of Quebec's most well-known celebrities disappeared from stages and television screens amid accusations of sexual impropriety.

All of the Canadian cases came after revelations last fall about the American film producer Harvey Weinstein set off a wave of accusations of sexual harassment and impropriety, with women speaking out loudly through the #MeToo movement and dozens of men resigning from their posts in entertainment, politics, publishing and journalism.

Canada had already been grappling with the issue of sexual assault in various cases through the years, but the volume of women's voices across the border gave many reason to believe that the climate in their country might have changed, too.

"It's a perfect storm for reform," said Michelle Coffin, a political science professor at Saint Mary's University in Halifax, Nova Scotia, who worked in provincial politics for more than five years.

It is not only that Canadian women feel emboldened by their American counterparts, she added. They also feel propelled by American politics, she said.

Women are speaking up to make sure "that we do not get to that place where we have a prime minister accused of sexual assault, where there's a tape of him talking about women in a misogynistic way," Professor Coffin said, referring to the "Access Hollywood" recording in which Donald J. Trump bragged about grabbing women's genitals.

Paulette Senior, president of the Canadian Women's Foundation, which finances gender equality projects across the country, said the election of Mr. Trump galvanized Canadian feminists, too.

"It woke up women out of their slumber, those of us, even me, who took it for granted that could never happen," Ms. Senior said. "We realized that all we have worked for can be lost."

Over the past week, as the accusations piled up, Canadian politicians from all parties have been swift to demand change and, even more unusually, publicly applaud female victims for disclosing their stories of abuse or assault, even anonymously.

Lisa Raitt, the deputy leader of the Conservative Party, called the women whose disclosures have toppled two provincial leaders from her own party "brave young women" on the national Canadian Broadcasting Corporation over the weekend. "I commend them for coming forward. Now, it's caused an awful lot of turmoil in politics, but that's O.K."

Rachel Notley, the premier of Alberta, put out a message on Facebookon Monday evening: "I say to everyone in Alberta who has been subject to sexual harassment, you have a right to tell your story and share your experience. And that right must come without fear of retribution. Any form of intimidation is wrong. Threats associated with speaking out are also wrong. Completely."

Ms. Notley's public announcement came after an Alberta political staff member last week on Twitter accused Kent Hehr, federal minister of sport and persons with disabilities, of making sexual comments about her, prompting his resignation. The staff member told various Canadian media outlets that after her accusations she received a barrage of death threats, including one slipped under her door at home.

Unlike the government in Washington, the federal government in Canada under Prime Minister Justin Trudeau, a self-described feminist, has been leading the push to address sexual harassment. The legislation his government introduced Monday defines it broadly, as any comment, gesture or touching "of a sexual nature" that could offend or humiliate an employee.

The bill also includes as sexual harassment any "condition of a sexual nature" that might affect a worker's job security or opportunities for promotion. If passed, the changes will set up a formal complaint system and give the labor department sweeping investigatory powers.

The proposed measure also extends the rules to political staff members for the first time. Over the past week, many former political staff members have told personal stories of unwanted groping, kissing and lewd comments they suffered so regularly they thought it was part of the job.

"Things need to change and it starts with saying emphatically that it is never O.K.," said Ms. Hajdu, the labor minister, on Monday. She said Parliament was "a place where often the victimized individual is blamed for the harassment that she herself has experienced. We are all familiar with this phrase: 'She brought it on herself.'"

The new definitions and complaint systems will, in practice, benefit a minority of Canadian workers — those who work in the federal government and in federally regulated businesses like banks, airlines and railways.

Just over three years ago, the debate over sexual harassment flared up in Canada after the firing and arrest of a prominent musician and radio host, Jian Ghomeshi. That brought the topic of sexual assault out from women's shelters into coffee shops and onto daily radio shows, where it has mostly remained.

But instead of emboldening other women, the spectacle of Mr. Ghomeshi's criminal trial proved to silence women. In declaring Mr. Ghomeshi not guilty, the judge described the female complainants as insincere and deceptive.

Now that the movement is back on its feet, Canadian feminists say, they hope the grass-roots movement catches up with the political leadership, and changes spread from politics and the media into other domains.

"It is a very interesting political time," said Lise Gotell, a professor of women and gender studies at the University of Alberta. "There is a lot of space for feminism. I certainly would not have predicted this."

CHAPTER 3

The Effects of #MeToo

The effects of #MeToo were sudden and diverse. Harvey Weinstein resigned from the company he founded. Dozens of other men left high-profile positions, some voluntarily, many by force. Gymnastics doctor Larry Nassar was condemned to as many as 175 years in prison for criminal sexual misconduct after more than 150 women confronted him at his sentencing hearing. Men began to question which of their actions may have been perceived as harassment and to consider how they could help enact social change. And 300 of Hollywood's most powerful women founded Time's Up, an organization designed to create an anti-harassment action plan.

Men at Work Wonder if They Overstepped With Women, Too

BY NELLIE BOWLES | NOV. 10, 2017

SAN FRANCISCO — It has been a confusing season for America's working men, as the conversation around workplace harassment reveals it to be a nationwide epidemic — and many men wonder if they were involved or ignored the signs.

Consider Owen Cunningham, a director at San Francisco's KBM-Hogue design firm. When he looks toward the annual corporate holiday party these days, he shudders.

"Cancel the holiday party," said Mr. Cunningham, 37, adding that he means just until it has been figured out how men and women should

It has been a confusing season for America's working men, as the conversation around workplace harassment reveals it to be a nationwide epidemic.

interact. He said he considered himself progresive on gender issues but was thinking more about the behavior he had seen in the past: "What flirting is O.K.? Was I ever taking advantage of any meager power I had? You start to wonder."

Across white-collar workplaces, rank-and-file men are awakening to the prevalence of sexual harassment and assault after high-profile cases including those of Harvey Weinstein, Mark Halperin and Louis C.K. Those cases helped inspire the #MeToo campaign, in which thousands of women have posted about their own harassment experiences on social media. Now many men who like to think they treat women as equals in the workplace are starting to look back at their own behavior and are wondering if they, too, have overstepped at work — in overt or subtle ways that would get them included in a #MeToo post.

"I don't think I've done anything wrong," said Nick Matthews, 42, who works at PwC, formerly PricewaterhouseCoopers, and lives in San Francisco. "But has anything I've done been interpreted another way?"

In response, some men are forming all-male text groups at companies or in their industries to brainstorm on harassment issues. Some said they planned to be a lot more careful in interacting with women because they felt that the line between friendliness and sexual harassment was too easy to cross. Others are struggling to reconcile how these behaviors could happen even among men who believe in equal rights.

Joel Milton, 30, an entrepreneur in Denver with Baker Technologies, a platform for cannabis dispensaries, said he had recently decided to be more careful about corporate offsites after seeing the swell of #MeToo claims.

"When I hear someone on my team is having a pool party, now I'll say, 'Hey, maybe no managers should be there,'" Mr. Milton said, relaying the type of information likely to be covered in many companies' employment manuals.

He added that harassment was not something he had thought much about before, but that he was considering his own behavior more. "Like, did I ever do anything?" he said.

Many companies have long mandated anti-harassment training to educate men and women about the issue. But in a report last year, the United States Equal Employment Opportunity Commission found that much of that training was ineffective and that workplace harassment was widely underreported.

Jonathan Segal, a lawyer who was on the commission's harassment task force, said he was now fielding odd questions from men about how to behave at work. At a fund-raiser last month in Palm Beach, Fla., some men asked him if it was permissible to hug a woman and where the boundaries should be drawn.

Mr. Segal said he had explained to the men that the context mattered and that pretending there was a gray zone between collegial friendliness and sexual assault was absurd. For instance, he told them, hugging an old friend is very different from going up behind a co-worker while she was at a desk typing.

Owen Cunningham, who works at a design firm in San Francisco, said he had started wondering, "What flirting is O.K.?"

"If someone can't understand that, then maybe they just shouldn't be hugging," he said.

Mr. Segal, who runs anti-harassment training, is now expanding part of the program called Safe Mentoring, which teaches men how to mentor younger women without harassing them. At a recent session, a male supervisor talked about having an extra ticket to a sporting event and feeling he could invite only a male colleague; Mr. Segal went over how to invite a female colleague without sexually harassing her.

"The answer to harassment cannot be avoiding women," he said.

Still, some workers said they were starting to follow "the Pence rule," which was formerly known as the Billy Graham rule, after the evangelical preacher, but is now named for Vice President Mike Pence. Mr. Pence has said he does not eat alone with women who are not his wife or attend an event without her if alcohol will be served.

A conservative writer, Sean Davis, wrote that a lot of men in media should have effectively been heeding the Pence rule all along. He said he had always followed it and that coastal, liberal America was finally waking up to how useful avoiding private meetings with women could be. The former White House adviser Sebastian Gorka also made this argument.

"What we're seeing now is men are backing away from the role that we try to encourage them to play, which is actively mentoring and sponsoring women in the workplace," said Al Harris, who has been running workplace equality programs and writing on the topic from Chicago with his partner, Andie Kramer, for many years. "There's apprehension on the part of men that they're going to be falsely accused of sexual harassment."

Not everyone is practicing avoidance. Some men said the best route is to ask female co-workers directly if they feel harassed. Pat Lencioni, the founder of the Table Group in Lafayette, Calif., which does executive coaching for companies around issues like diversity, said he was doing just that and had asked the women at his office if they worried about harassment.

"I came into the office and said, 'Hey, guys, I've got a question for you: This sexual harassment stuff, all these things, do you guys ever worry it's going to happen here?'" Mr. Lencioni, 52, recalled. "And they were like: 'No, because we know you. We know who you are.'"

He said he thought this approach could be adopted more broadly.

Other men said they had not talked about workplace harassment with anyone because they already knew what they needed to know. "This is a liberal town," said Philip Rontell, a real estate agent in Walnut Creek, Calif., who added that he supported the #MeToo campaign. "We all already know this stuff."

When men do want to talk about workplace harassment, some said, they don't know where to go. "I just don't know where those conversations are allowed to be had," said Ryan Ellis, 33, a sales manager for an e-commerce company in Santa Monica, Calif.

Austin Gilbert, a recruiter in San Francisco for the company Gametime, said his industry had also had to deal with men talking in online chat rooms at work, which he said could "bury" and hide toxic comments. His company has closed several "high school in-group" type of exclusionary work chats over the years, but he worries about more.

"We have a policy of telling employees that we're free to review all electronic communications," Mr. Gilbert, 31, said. "But that's typically not anyone's job responsibility in a small company."

With women empowered to call out inappropriate behavior, some companies predict that boozy after-work events for the holidays could be combustible this year. While many companies used to have the parties on Thursday or Friday evenings, some are moving them to late Monday or Tuesday afternoons, said Sarah Freedman, the vice president of operations for 23 Layers, an event planner in New York whose clients include Google and West Elm.

Open bars are being replaced with game zones. One client recently asked for an extremely watered-down "John Daly" to be the party's signature drink, which Ms. Freeman found strange but probably wise.

After-work events are "the front line" when it comes to harassment, and companies want "more safety precautions" now, she said.

Gymnastics Doctor Who Abused Patients Gets 60 Years for Child Pornography

BY MAGGIE ASTOR | DEC. 7, 2017

DR. LAWRENCE G. NASSAR, a former team doctor for U.S.A. Gymnastics who has pleaded guilty to sexually abusing gymnasts under the guise of medical treatment, was sentenced on Thursday to 60 years in prison on child pornography charges.

The charges, which stemmed from more than 37,000 images of child pornography found on Dr. Nassar's computer, are separate from the 10 molestation counts on which sentences will be handed down in January. He pleaded guilty to the pornography charges over the summer, and to the molestation charges in November.

Dr. Nassar, 54, is expected to be sentenced to 25 years or more on the molestation charges. But even without that, he is virtually certain to spend the rest of his life in prison after Janet T. Neff, a federal district judge in Grand Rapids, Mich., imposed three consecutive 20-year sentences in the child pornography case.

Matthew Newburg, a lawyer for Dr. Nassar, declined to comment on Thursday.

The case against Dr. Nassar emerged last year, after an Indianapolis Star investigation found that U.S.A. Gymnastics, the sport's national governing body, had systematically failed to report gymnasts' allegations of sexual abuse by coaches. Then, in September 2016, The Star published detailed accounts from two former gymnasts who said that, among other sexually abusive behavior, Dr. Nassar had penetrated them with his fingers, claiming it was a treatment for back pain.

Those two gymnasts — Rachael Denhollander, who was the first to step forward by name, and Jamie Dantzscher, who initially remained anonymous but later spoke out publicly — broke a dam of silence in the sport, more than a year before the #MeToo movement began revealing sexual misconduct by innumerable men in powerful positions. More than 130 women — mostly but not exclusively gymnasts — have now described abuse by Dr. Nassar (who worked both for the national team and for Michigan State University). Among them are at least seven former members of the United States national gymnastics team, including four Olympians.

Many of the women submitted victim impact statements to the court before the sentencing on Thursday. Judge Neff ruled last week that they could not be read aloud in the courtroom, but some women shared their statements through other channels.

McKayla Maroney, a 2012 Olympian who came forward in October as one of Dr. Nassar's victims, wrote in her statement that he "deserves to spend the rest of his life in prison."

"He abused my trust, abused my body and left scars on my psyche that may never heal," Ms. Maroney wrote, according to ESPN.

And Aly Raisman — the captain of the American women's gymnastics teams at the 2012 and 2016 Olympics, and one of the most outspoken survivors of Dr. Nassar's abuse — published thousands of words in The Players' Tribune on Thursday.

"I ask that you give Larry the strongest possible sentence (which his actions deserve), for by doing so, you will send a message to him and to other abusers that they cannot get away with their horrible crimes," Ms. Raisman, 23, said in her statement. "Maybe knowing that Larry is being held accountable for his abuse will help me and the other survivors feel less alone, like we're being heard, and open up pathways for healing."

Because of Dr. Nassar's abuse, Ms. Raisman wrote, she is frequently afraid: afraid that other doctors will treat her similarly; afraid even that a man will deliver her room service order when she travels.

"I hold the door open as he drops off the food and keep it open until he leaves," she wrote. "I often wonder if I am hurting their feelings by being so obviously distrusting of them. I always used to give people the benefit of the doubt, but if a decorated doctor who served on the national team for over 30 years turned out to be a monster, then how can I trust anybody?"

Even so, she continued: "I am not a victim. I am a survivor. The abuse does not define me, or anyone else who has been abused."

Beyond Dr. Nassar himself, the cases have ensnared U.S.A. Gymnastics and many of its top officials, whom lawsuits have accused of turning a blind eye and of fostering toxic environments in which abuse could flourish. Earlier this year, U.S.A. Gymnastics adopted stricter reporting policies in response to an extensive report on its previous failings.

Some gymnasts said it was difficult to feel entirely victorious after the sentencing, because Dr. Nassar was part of a much larger problem.

"Today, the justice feels very incomplete," Ms. Denhollander said at a news conference on Thursday.

Larry Nassar Is Sentenced to Another 40 to 125 Years in Prison

BY CHRISTINE HAUSER | FEB. 5, 2018

LAWRENCE G. NASSAR, the former U.S.A. Gymnastics and Michigan State University sports medicine doctor, was sentenced in a Michigan court on Monday to 40 to 125 years in prison for criminal sexual conduct toward girls at a gymnastics facility.

Judge Janice K. Cunningham announced the sentence in Eaton County Circuit Court in Charlotte, Mich., at the end of a sentencing hearing in which more than 60 young women and teenagers read or presented victim impact statements.

The sentence was based on Dr. Nassar's November guilty plea to three counts of criminal sexual conduct, two of them against girls between the ages of 13 and 15, and one against a girl younger than 13. The abuse took place at Twistars Gymnastics Club, outside Lansing, Mich., between September 2009 and September 2011, the plea agreement said.

The gym was supposed to catapult young female athletes to fruitful careers under the guidance of John Geddert, who owned the gym and coached there. Mr. Geddert coached the U.S. Olympic team in 2012.

Judge Cunningham said the depth and tragedy of the case was incomprehensible. "It spans the country, and the world," she said. "It has impacted women, children and families of varying ages, races and walks of life. Individuals that have suffered physical and emotional harm as a result of your actions live all over the country and the world."

Dr. Nassar, in a final statement, said that he was sorry, and that the words of the young women and parents "impacted me to my innermost core." But he added that he knew "it pales in comparison to the pain, trauma and emotions that you all feel."

The sentencing in Eaton County marked the end of weeks of emotional statements by young women and girls who said they were abused by Dr. Nassar under the guise of medical treatment. Judge Cunningham said on the first day of the hearing that the number of victims who had come forward had risen to 265, some of whom have chosen to remain anonymous.

Last month, more than 150 of them publicly confronted him during a seven-day hearing in Ingham County Circuit Court in Lansing, where he had pleaded guilty in November to seven counts of sexual assault. Among them were Olympic athletes including Aly Raisman and Jordyn Wieber.

He was sentenced to 40 to 175 years for the charges in Ingham County, and 60 years for a conviction related to child pornography in a separate federal case.

The Eaton County sentence will be served concurrently with the Ingham County sentence but after the child pornography sentence, the judge said.

The abuse came to light after an Indianapolis Star investigationin 2016 reported accusations against Dr. Nassar that went back decades. The case has reverberated far beyond the courtrooms of Michigan, leading to efforts to identify the officials who knew about the abuse and covered it up.

The New York Times identified at least 40 girls and women who say that Dr. Nassar molested them between July 2015, when he fell under F.B.I. scrutiny, and September 2016, when he was exposed by the Indianapolis Star investigation.

U.S.A. Gymnastics, the sport's governing body, has been widely derided for its handling of the scandal. Last month, its entire board of directors stepped down after the United States Olympic Committee threatened it with decertification.

The case has also prompted a shake-up within M.S.U., Dr. Nassar's former employer. Its longtime president, Lou Anna Simon, resigned last month, and the board of trustees voted unanimously to name John Engler, the former governor of Michigan, as its interim president. But Mr. Engler's appointment was met with student protests, and the trustees are facing a possible no-confidence vote by the faculty, the Lansing State Journal reported.

Rachael Denhollander, who filed a police report in August 2016 accusing Dr. Nassar of sexually abusing her when she was 15 years old and became the first woman to be named publicly in the case, described the case on Monday as "the greatest sexual assault scandal in history," according to a report by The Associated Press.

The victims, she added, "wouldn't be here had the adults and authorities done what they should have done 20 years ago."

Mea Culpa. Kinda Sorta.

BY THE NEW YORK TIMES | DEC. 1, 2017

New York Times journalists analyze the apologies — and non-apologies— issued by high-profile men accused of sexual misconduct.

ON THURSDAY it was Matt Lauer, the longtime host of the "Today" show, expressing "sorrow and regret for the pain I have caused," the day after NBC News fired him over allegations of sexual misconduct.

Three days earlier Al Franken, a Minnesota Democrat, issued his third apology since a radio broadcaster accused him of forcibly kissing her and groping her breasts. Before that it was Louis C.K., the ribald comedian accused of serially masturbating in front of colleagues, whose 493-word statement did not include the word "sorry." Roy Moore, the Republican Senate candidate in Alabama, outright denied that he groped teenaged girls, calling the allegations "dirty politics."

The powerful men felled by sexual misconduct allegations over the past two months have had a range of responses. Below, four New York Times journalists — Jessica Bennett, our new gender editor; Claire Cain Miller, who writes about gender in the workplace for The Upshot; Amanda Taub, co-author of The Interpreter column and newsletter; and Choire Sicha, our Styles editor — dissect five of these statements, analyzing both what is there and what might be missing.

CHARLIE ROSE, NOV. 20

The longtime television host was accused by eight women of harassing them — with nudity, groping and lewd calls:

In my 45 years in journalism, I have prided myself on being an advocate for the careers of the women with whom I have worked.

One of the great paradoxes of so many of these men (and in so many of these cases) is that being an advocate for women does not in fact mean that you can't ALSO be a serial harasser.

JESSICA BENNETT, GENDER EDITOR

Nevertheless, in the past few days, claims have been made about my behavior toward some former female colleagues.

This tactic — "Oh I am also surprised to hear these allegations!" — looks like part denial and part arrogance. Women started crying when he touched them! That's a sign that your touch is bad touch, just F.Y.I.

CHOIRE SICHA, STYLES EDITOR

It is essential that these women know I hear them and that I deeply apologize for my inappropriate behavior. I am greatly embarrassed. I have behaved insensitively at times, and I accept responsibility for that, though I do not believe that all of these allegations are accurate. I always felt that I was pursuing shared feelings, even though I now realize I was mistaken.

All the hedging makes it seem as if he doesn't yet fully accept responsibility.

CLAIRE CAIN MILLER, REPORTER, THE UPSHOT

I have learned a great deal as a result of these events, and I hope others will too. All of us, including me, are coming to a newer and deeper recognition of the pain caused by conduct in the past, and have come to a profound new respect for women and their lives.

How nice that women's suffering could be a learning experience for the man who harassed them.

AMANDA TAUB, COLUMNIST, THE INTERPRETER

AL FRANKEN, NOV. 17

Senator Franken, Democrat of Minnesota, was accused of kissing a radio broadcaster without her consent, and photographed groping her breast while she slept:

The first thing I want to do is apologize: to Leeann, to everyone else who was part of that tour, to everyone who has worked for me, to everyone I represent, and to everyone who counts on me to be an ally and supporter and champion of women. There's more I want to say, but the first and most important thing — and if it's the only thing you care to hear, that's fine — is: I'm sorry.

It should perhaps not be worth noting, but in the context of so many of these statements it is: that Senator Franken uses the actual words "I'm sorry" in his apology.

JESSICA BENNETT, GENDER EDITOR

I respect women. I don't respect men who don't. And the fact that my own actions have given people a good reason to doubt that makes me feel ashamed.

But I want to say something else, too. Over the last few months, all of us — including and especially men who respect women — **have been forced to take a good, hard look at our own actions** *and think (perhaps, shamefully, for the first time) about how those actions have affected women.*

This gets at one of the underlying issues: Will things actually improve if men don't realize this behavior is wrong until they are "forced" — by brave women and by investigative reporters — to address their actions publicly?

CLAIRE CAIN MILLER, REPORTER, THE UPSHOT

For instance, that picture. I don't know what was in my head when I took that picture, and it doesn't matter. **There's no excuse.**

This declaration is one reason I think that, as a whole, his apology seems more genuine than many of them.

CLAIRE CAIN MILLER, REPORTER, THE UPSHOT

I look at it now and I feel disgusted with myself. It isn't funny. It's completely inappropriate. It's obvious how Leeann would feel violated by that picture. And, what's more, I can see how millions of other women would feel violated by it — women who have had similar experiences in their own lives, women who fear having those experiences, women who look up to me, women who have counted on me.

Coming from the world of comedy, **I've told and written a lot of jokes that I once thought were funny but later came to realize were just plain offensive.** *But the intentions behind my actions aren't the point at all. It's the impact these jokes had on others that matters. And I'm sorry it's taken me so long to come to terms with that.*

This is a point that many of the other apologies failed to grasp.

AMANDA TAUB, COLUMNIST, THE INTERPRETER

*While I don't remember the rehearsal for the skit as Leeann does, I under-
stand why we need to listen to and believe women's experiences.*

"I remember it differently" is a classic excuse for this behavior — but
he saves it by saying that regardless, the women should be believed.

CLAIRE CAIN MILLER, REPORTER, THE UPSHOT

*I am asking that ethics investigation be undertaken, and I will gladly
cooperate. And the truth is, what people think of me in light of this is far less
important than what people think of women who continue to come forward to tell their stories. They deserve to be heard, and believed. And they
deserve to know that I am their ally and supporter. I have let them down
and am committed to making it up to them.*

LOUIS C.K., NOV. 10

The comedian was accused by five women of sexual misconduct,
including masturbating in front of them:

*I want to address the stories told to The New York Times by five women
named Abby, Rebecca, Dana, Julia who felt able to name themselves and
one who did not.*

 *These stories are true. At the time, I said to myself that what I did was
O.K. because I never showed a woman my dick without asking first, which
is also true. But what I learned later in life, too late, is that **when you
have power over another person, asking them to look at your dick isn't a
question.***

This is exactly right, and a lesson I hope gets learned from all of these
stories: When you're in power, consent is not straightforward.

CLAIRE CAIN MILLER, REPORTER, THE UPSHOT

*It's a predicament for them. The power I had over these women is that they
admired me. And I wielded that power irresponsibly. I have been remorseful
of my actions. And I've tried to learn from them. And run from them. Now
I'm aware of the extent of the impact of my actions. I learned yesterday
the extent to which I left these women who **admired me** feeling badly about
themselves and cautious around other men who would never have put them
in that position.*

Louis C.K. mentions that his victims "admired" him no fewer than four times in this apology. But his power in these situations went beyond admiration. He was a successful comedian with a powerful manager, which meant he had power and influence in the comedy industry at large.

AMANDA TAUB, COLUMNIST, THE INTERPRETER

*I also took advantage of the fact that I was widely admired in my and their community, which disabled them from sharing their story and brought hardship to them when they tried because people who look up to me didn't want to hear it. I didn't think that I was doing any of that **because my position allowed me not to think about it.** There is nothing about this that I forgive myself for. And I have to reconcile it with who I am. Which is nothing compared to the task I left them with. I wish I had reacted to their admiration of me by being a good example to them as a man and given them some guidance as a comedian, including because I admired their work.*

He's unsuccessfully trying to express an interesting idea here. I don't believe that he didn't think about what he did with women, particularly as people were trying to get this story out for years, or else, for one thing, he wouldn't have literally written a movie ("I Love You, Daddy") about how older men are totally powerless around alluring women. In any event there's something no one has yet untangled here, about the denial and mental machinations of these men. But 100 percent they thought about it, all the time, even when they shut it out in the day-to-day to focus on their most important mission, building their careers.

CHOIRE SICHA, STYLES EDITOR

The hardest regret to live with is what you've done to hurt someone else. And I can hardly wrap my head around the scope of hurt I brought on them. I'd be remiss to exclude the hurt that I've brought on people who I work with and have worked with who's professional and personal lives have been impacted by all of this, including projects currently in production:

One often hears people talk about this kind of damage as a consequence of victims going public, or harassers being punished, rather than consequences of the harassment itself. Good for Louis C.K. for acknowledging that these consequences flow from his own actions.

AMANDA TAUB, COLUMNIST, THE INTERPRETER

I have spent my long and lucky career talking and saying anything I want. I will now step back and take a long time to listen. Thank you for reading.

KEVIN SPACEY, OCT. 30

The two-time Oscar winner was accused of molesting a 14-year-old boy:

I have a lot of respect and admiration for Anthony Rapp as an actor. I'm beyond horrified to hear this story. I honestly do not remember the encounter, it would have been over 30 years ago. But if I did behave then as he describes, I owe him the sincerest apology for what would have been deeply inappropriate drunken behavior, and I am sorry for the feelings he describes having carried with him all these years.

This story has encouraged me to address other things about my life. I know that there are stories out there about me and that some have been fueled by the fact that I have been so protective of my privacy. As those closest to me know, in my life I have had relationships with both men and women. **I have loved and had romantic encounters with men throughout my life, and I choose now to live as a gay man.** *I want to deal with this honestly and openly and that starts with examining my own behavior.*

As many have noted, Mr. Spacey's decision to bring up his sexuality in the context of his apology seems like savvy deflection. It gave the media a different story to report, and by framing his treatment of Mr. Rapp as part of his romantic involvements, he implies that criticism of it is rooted in homophobia. Many found this statement particularly odious because it draws on harmful stereotypes of gay men as sexual predators who endanger children.

AMANDA TAUB, COLUMNIST, THE INTERPRETER

HARVEY WEINSTEIN, OCT. 5

The Hollywood titan was fired from his production company after investigations in The New York Times and New Yorker found he had sexually harassed, assaulted and attempted to pay off many women:

I came of age in the 60's and 70's, when all the rules about behavior and workplaces were different.

As many people have pointed out, this is absolutely false. Never was his behavior acceptable. (Not to mention the fact that his behavior continued well past that time period.)

CLAIRE CAIN MILLER, REPORTER, THE UPSHOT

I realized some time ago that I needed to be a better person and my interactions with the people I work with have changed. I appreciate the way I've behaved with colleagues in the past has caused a lot of pain, and I sincerely apologize for it.

Though I'm trying to do better, I know I have a long way to go. That is my commitment. My journey now will be to learn about myself and conquer my demons.

Another apology that frames consequences for misbehavior as a learning experience.

AMANDA TAUB, COLUMNIST, THE INTERPRETER

Over the last year I've asked Lisa Bloom to tutor me and she's put together a team of people. I've brought on therapists and I plan to take a leave of absence from my company and to deal with this issue head on. I so respect all the women and regret what happened. I hope that my actions will speak louder than words and that one day we will all be able to earn their trust and sit down together with Lisa to learn more.

I've always wondered if this meant he hired full-time therapists on, like, his personal staff. And if he did so, did he yell at them and bully them like any other Weinstein staff member in history? Does Bob get to yell at them too? How does this work?

CHOIRE SICHA, STYLES EDITOR

Jay-Z wrote in 4:44: "I'm not the man I thought I was and I better be that man for my children." The same is true for me. I want a second chance in

the community but I know I've got work to do to earn it. I have goals that
are now priorities. Trust me, this isn't an overnight process. I've been trying
to do this for 10 years and this is a wake-up call. I cannot be more remorse-
ful about the people I hurt and I plan to do right by all of them.

As many have now noted, this is a misquote. The closest thing Jay-Z says to this in 4:44 is: "And if my children knew / I don't even know what I would do."

JESSICA BENNETT, GENDER EDITOR

I am going to need a place to channel that anger so I've decided I'm going
to give the NRA my full attention. I hope Wayne LaPierre will enjoy his
retirement party.

Interpreting this paragraph would require far greater psychiatric expertise than I have, but to start, why exactly would we care about HIS anger at this moment?

CLAIRE CAIN MILLER, REPORTER, THE UPSHOT

I'm going to do it at the same place I did my Bar Mitzvah.
I'm making a movie about our President, perhaps we can make it a joint
retirement party. One year ago, I began organizing a $5 million foundation
to give scholarships to women directors at USC. While this might seem coin-
cidental, it has been in the works for a year. It will be named after my mom
and I won't disappoint her.

These sound like the ramblings of your crazy uncle at Thanksgiving dinner.

JESSICA BENNETT, GENDER EDITOR

Alabama Women 'Make a Stand' in First Election of the #MeToo Era

BY JESS BIDGOOD | DEC. 13, 2017

BIRMINGHAM, ALA. — For Janet Maycock, Tuesday's election of the Democrat Doug Jones in Alabama was personal.

The allegations of sexual misconduct against teenage girls by Mr. Jones's opponent, Roy S. Moore, the conservative former judge, had stoked Ms. Maycock's own memories of being molested by an older employee in the restaurant where she worked when she was 17, and of feeling like she could never speak up about it

"It made me more adamant to keep a man like that out of the Senate," said Ms. Maycock, 67, who is black and was among numerous women celebrating at Mr. Jones's victory party. She wanted, she said, "to make a stand for women who have the courage to speak out."

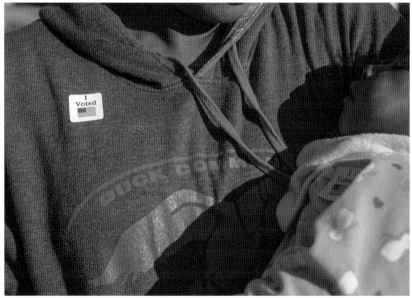

An Alabama voter at a polling station in Dothan on Tuesday. Exit polls suggested that a majority of women backed Doug Jones, the Democratic candidate.

Depending on one's point of view, Tuesday's election was a referendum on decency, a test of the credibility of the news media, or a rallying cry against outside interference in Alabama politics. But it was also the first election in the #MeToo era and a measure of the deep divide among women over personal issues like sexual harassment, religion and race.

Exit polls conducted by Edison Research for the National Election Pool suggested a majority of women, 57 percent, backed Mr. Jones, compared with 42 percent of men. But the polls also showed women as sharply divided by race, with about 98 percent of black women supporting Mr. Jones, mobilizing heavily to carry out a long tradition of supporting Democrats here.

Among white women, 34 percent supported Mr. Jones, according to the polls. In 2012, the last presidential election in which an exit poll was conducted in Alabama — which is not usually a battleground state — President Barack Obama won only 16 percent of white women.

Many of Mr. Moore's supporters, like Deborah Webb, a white nurse from Centreville, Ala., dismissed the allegations against him up until the end, focusing instead on his religious credentials.

"God, country, military, that's what we love," said Ms. Webb, 54, adding, "As a Christian, I want to vote for someone who has those values, someone who loves the Lord."

Mr. Moore had the support of prominent female Republicans in the state, including Gov. Kay Ivey, who said she believed his accusers but would vote for him anyway, and Terry Lathan, the chairwoman of the Alabama Republican Party.

"Party identity is the key to the white vote" regardless of gender, said Natalie Davis, a professor emerita at Birmingham-Southern College. And on Tuesday, many women cast a vote for the party, even if the allegations left them uneasy. "I wasn't sure who to vote for, even though I'm a Republican," said Brandy McDonald, 40, a hairstylist who is white, as she left a church polling place in Hoover. She said she had only made her final decision to vote for Mr. Moore that morning.

Marie Owen waited for a ride after voting in Blount County, Ala. "I voted for Moore, but I hope for the good. Whatever it is. I just want us to get back to like it used to be," she said.

Still, women did provide Mr. Jones's margin of victory. "There's no doubt about that," said David Wasserman, an editor for the Cook Political Report, adding that Mr. Jones's victory was also driven by the high turnout among black voters of both genders and college-educated voters.

The rejection of Mr. Moore by women stretched well beyond major cities like Birmingham and Montgomery, coursing into places like Ozark, the seat of Dale County, in the heart of the Wiregrass region that is ordinarily a Republican stronghold.

There, Tanya Embry, 36, who is white, cast her ballot for Mr. Jones at a civic center in southeast Alabama. "I know this is typically a Republican state, but I can't get behind somebody who is being accused of things like what he's being accused of," Ms. Embry said.

Seth C. McKee, an associate professor of political science at Texas Tech University who studies American elections, said the gap Tuesday among white men and women in Alabama was particularly noteworthy.

Claudia Anderson, right, and her son De'Mon Anderson, leaving the polls in Ozark, Ala., on Tuesday.

"In the South, there usually isn't any," Mr. McKee said. In exit polls, nine percentage points separated white men, who went for Mr. Moore by 72 percent, and white women, who went for Mr. Moore by 63 percent, yet he had been banking on even more support from female voters.

In Gadsden, Ala., where Mr. Moore was accused of making unwanted advances to women, Melissa Simmons, 32, and Donzella Williams, 40, stood outside a polling place hoping to make a last-minute pitch to voters. Both of them, who are black, said they were appalled by the allegations against Mr. Moore, and spoke of them in the context of raising their children: What sort of message would it carry, they said, to send that sort of man to the Senate?

"Guys are going to think they can do these kinds of things to women, and think, 'We can get away with it,'" Ms. Williams said. "And Trump is basically telling Roy Moore, 'It's O.K., I did the same thing. You'll get into office and you can push it under the rug.'"

Other women, like Ms. Maycock in Birmingham, who volunteered for Mr. Jones, went to the polls and voted for him with their own painful histories in mind. Casie Baker, 29, said she had been molested as a child, and understood why the allegations had taken so long to surface. "This is nothing against Roy Moore," she said, "but I personally have dealt with being molested myself, and I know it can take a long time before you can say something."

Still, after voting in Hoover, Madeleine Bell-Colpack, 19, who is white, took a moment to celebrate, stopping on the church steps to take a selfie in the cold night air. Her vote for Mr. Jones, she said, was a repudiation of a sexually aggressive culture reflected in the allegations against Mr. Moore.

"I'm from Alabama. The culture is rampant," Ms. Bell-Colpack said. "That's why this election was so important to me — we have to get away from that."

Some women at Mr. Jones's election night party in Birmingham, where campaign volunteers and devoted supporters cheered beneath confetti, were quick to caution that his victory was not won solely upon the allegations against Mr. Moore.

"In Alabama, we are looking at a bigger picture than what the nation was looking at," said Sandra Chandler, 50, a black mother of three who said education was the driving issue for her.

Zarinah Shahid, 34, a project manager who lives in Birmingham and is black, said Mr. Jones's victory nevertheless felt like a leap forward for women, and a culmination of a new burst of Democratic energy that emerged here after the election of President Trump last year.

"I thought about going to the Women's March, and seeing where we've come from there," Ms. Shahid said. "It means everything for us."

RICHARD FAUSSET CONTRIBUTED REPORTING FROM GADSDEN, ALA., AND ALAN BLINDER FROM OZARK, ALA. PATRICIA MAZZEI CONTRIBUTED REPORTING FROM NEW YORK.

The Politics of #HimToo

OPINION | BY THOMAS B. EDSALL | DEC. 14, 2017

THE ISSUE of sexual misconduct has emerged as a centerpiece of Democratic strategy for taking on President Trump and the Republican Party. That strategy paid off on Tuesday with the defeat of Roy Moore.

Senator Kirsten Gillibrand's decision to bring to center stage charges of sexual harassment leveled by more than a dozen women against Trump has forced the White House onto the defensive.

THE STORY SO FAR

On Sunday, Nikki Haley, Trump's ambassador to the United Nations, broke ranks with the administration, telling John Dickerson on "Face the Nation" that Trump's accusers "should be heard. They should be heard and they should be dealt with." Haley added that she is "incredibly proud of the women who have come forward" in all the recent cases of alleged harassment.

On Monday, three of Trump's accusers appeared on NBC Today with Megyn Kelly, following the publication of articles further chronicling Trump's alleged misconduct in People, The New Yorker, The Atlantic and New York magazine. The liberal filmmaker, Robert Greenwald, released a documentary, "16 Women and Donald Trump: Hear Their Stories."

All of these developments are taking place against the backdrop of a pending defamation lawsuit against Trump, who awaits the decision of Jennifer G. Schecter — a New York state judge — who is considering a motion to require Trump to testify under oath in a lawsuit brought by Summer Zervos, a former "Apprentice" contestant.

Zervos, who is represented by Gloria Allred, claims that in 2007 Trump "kissed her on the mouth repeatedly, touched her breast and pressed his genitals against her," without her consent. Zervos contends that she was defamed when Trump dismissed her claims during the campaign as "lies" and "nonsense."

Since the first week of October, when The Times wrote about Harvey Weinstein's pattern of sexual abuse, the floodwaters have been rising. At least 51 prominent men have been accused of sexual misconduct, ranging from groping to rape. The accused — many of them abruptly removed from their positions — run the ideological and partisan gamut from Garrison Keillor to Leon Wieseltier to John Conyers to Matt Lauer to James Levine to Trent Franks to Al Franken to Charlie Rose and on and on, including, most recently, Mario Batali and Russell Simmons.

For Democrats, who have struggled to find traction in their battles with the administration, the explosion of allegations has created an opening to put the focus on Trump — a development greatly enhanced by the Moore debacle.

Among Democrats, Gillibrand stands out as the politician who first claimed ownership of the issue, and she is seen by many analysts and commentators as having moved into the front ranks of potential presidential candidates. But what Gillibrand started has become a broader movement encompassing almost the entire Democratic Senate caucus.

After initiating the call on Franken to resign his seat, Gillibrand swiftly received remarkably strong support from her colleagues: 32 fellow Democratic senators and the two independent senators who caucus with the Democrats. There seemed to be an emerging consensus with a basic chess tactic: Sometimes you are required to sacrifice a pawn to checkmate the king.

In other words, Democrats smell blood, Trump's blood.

Gillibrand now says that Bill Clinton, one of her most steadfast supporters, should have resigned the presidency after his affair with Monica Lewinsky was revealed, and on Monday Gillibrand told CNN that Trump should leave office in the face of "very credible allegations of misconduct and criminal activity."

"I think when we start having to talk about the differences between sexual assault and sexual harassment and unwanted groping, you are having the wrong conversation," Gillibrand asserted at a news conference on Dec. 6. "You need to draw a line in the sand and say none of it is O.K. None of it is acceptable."

Gillibrand continued:

We, as elected leaders, should absolutely be held to a higher standard, not a lower standard, and we should fundamentally be valuing women, and that is where this debate has to go.

On Wednesday, Trump did Gillibrand a favor, tweeting:

Lightweight Senator Kirsten Gillibrand, a total flunky for Chuck Schumer and someone who would come to my office "begging" for campaign contributions not so long ago (and would do anything for them), is now in the ring fighting against Trump. Very disloyal to Bill & Crooked-USED!

USA Today, a publication known for the moderation and balance of its commentary, promptly editorialized:

A president who would all but call Sen. Kirsten Gillibrand a whore is not fit to clean the toilets in the Barack Obama Presidential Library or to shine the shoes of George W. Bush.

Kathleen Hall Jamieson, an expert on political rhetoric who is the director of the Annenberg Public Policy Center at the University of Pennsylvania, told Ashley Parker of the Washington Post that

there were striking parallels between Trump's Tuesday tweet and his comments in the "Access Hollywood" tape revealed during the campaign in which Trump boasts about grabbing women's genitals.

"In the 'Access Hollywood' tape, he says, 'You can do anything,' and in the tweet attacking Gillibrand, he says, she 'would do anything,'" Jamieson said:

What that language suggests is that the language for Trump is sexual language. We know he uses that language in a sexual context.

One of the strongest arguments in favor of a no-exceptions policy is that if Democrats want to capitalize on the surge of support for the #MeToo movement — and to make use of these issues against Trump and the likes of Roy Moore — they must have clean hands.

On Dec. 7, the Pew Research Center released results showing that in our highly polarized era, there is widespread bipartisan concern over sexual harassment, as the chart below shows.

Abby K. Wood, a professor of law, political science and public policy at the University of Southern California, made the following case in an email:

I'm struck by where the Democrats drew this line. Suppose they had drawn it somewhere between the allegations against Rep. John Conyers and those against Sen. Franken. By requesting retirement from Conyers but continuing to work with Franken, the message would have been that women should simply learn to live with some level of sexual harassment and assault. Instead, they seem to have drawn a bold line: no unwanted touching of any kind is permissible, full stop.

Many women, myself included, have been grabbed the way Senator Franken is alleged to have grabbed his victims. To be told — by a political party, no less — that we should no longer expect or tolerate that kind of behavior has the potential to be wildly empowering.

Blame for Sexual Harassment

Percentage of Americans who say recent allegations of sexual harassment and assault:

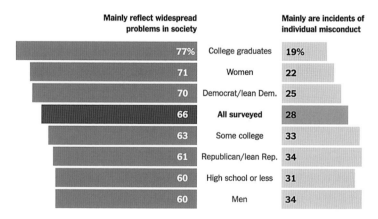

Mainly reflect widespread problems in society		Mainly are incidents of individual misconduct
77%	College graduates	19%
71	Women	22
70	Democrat/lean Dem.	25
66	**All surveyed**	28
63	Some college	33
61	Republican/lean Rep.	34
60	High school or less	31
60	Men	34

Chart does not include respondents who said they didn't know.

By The New York Times | Source: Pew Research Center survey conducted Nov. 29-Dec. 4

Jennifer Lawless, a political scientist at American University, agreed on most points with Wood. In an email, she wrote:

I can think only of pluses when considering the Democrats' strong stand against sexual harassment.

Not only can Democrats claim the moral high ground, Lawless argued, but they

differentiate themselves from the Republicans on an issue that is not wholly partisan. Doing so provides an opportunity — especially in swing states — to appeal to independents and even some moderate Republican women.

Not every supporter of zero tolerance is convinced that it will help win over wavering Republican voters.

Samara Klar, a professor of government and public policy at the University of Arizona, wrote by email that the attitudes of Republican women suggest deep partisan distrust of all things Democratic. Exit polls in Alabama showed Moore winning among white women by 29 percentage points, and carrying white women with college degrees by 7 points, although it is worth noting, as the veteran Republican operative Matthew Dowd did, that "when you break out evangelical vs non you get evangelical white women 76-22 Moore; non-evangelical white women 74-21 Jones!"

Nonetheless, Klar's research shows that:

For Democratic women, feminism is very closely aligned with being a woman. 55 percent of Democratic women say that the term "feminist" describes them "very well" or "extremely well." Only 10 percent of Republican women agree with that. Over 60 percent of Republican women say "feminist" describes them "not very well" or "not at all" — only 15 percent of Democratic women agree with that. In fact, 35 percent of Democratic men identify with the term "feminist" — more than triple the percent of Republican women who do so.

Klar's conclusion:

The Democrats are not likely to win over any Republican women based on their rejection of Franken and sexual harassment. This does not appear to be as much of a priority for Republican voters.

Seth Masket, a political scientist at the University of Denver, noted that

it's no easy thing for Democrats to cast aside longstanding party leaders, but at the same time, those leaders are more expendable than Republican leaders are. Al Franken and John Conyers can easily be replaced by other Democrats, and it costs Democrats nothing to turn against Bill Clinton. Donald Trump is president.

The other big plus for Democrats, according to Masket, is that the sexual harassment issue has put the Republican Party in the position

of playing fast and loose with moral and legal rectitude, which have long been advantageous topics for them.

It is now the Democrats who are drawing clear lines and saying that certain behaviors are unacceptable and must not be tolerated, while Republicans are sounding like moral relativists who will tolerate anything from people who will vote their way.

Christina Wolbrecht, a political scientist at Notre Dame, made the case in an email that inaction on Franken on the part of Democrats could have had a severe negative impact:

Failing to act on Franken might well have disheartened and disillusioned the activist base that the party desperately needs. This is not a question of turning Republican voters into Democratic voters, but rather of encouraging progressive voters to not just vote Democratic, but to direct their activism, donations, and energy through the party and for its candidates.

Still, there is a wide range of opinion on issues of sexual behavior within liberal ranks, including Emily Yoffe writing in Politico, Robert Kuttner writing in the American Prospect and Paul Rosenberg in Salon.

In her essay, "Why the #MeToo Moment Should Be Ready for a Backlash," Yoffe wrote:

This amazing moment has a chance to be truly transformative. But it could also go off track if all accusations are taken on faith, if due process is seen as an impediment rather than a requirement and an underpinning of justice, and if men and women grow wary of each other in the workplace.

"Shame on the Democrats for this stampede," Kuttner wrote:

Instead of turning on one of their own, Democrats and feminists — and all decent people — should be intensifying the pressure for a full investigation of the Groper-in-Chief.

Rosenberg, in turn, declared that a

Democratic rush to judgment, casting due process to the wind, in order to strike a virtue-signaling pose that almost surely will look increasingly dark in years to come.

In the heat of this intra-Democratic debate, some detect the potential for what they see as a more nuanced approach to the problem.

Elizabeth Bartholet, the director of the child advocacy program and a professor at Harvard Law School, who is no fan of Donald Trump, wrote in an email:

I think this is another moment we may look back on as a moment characterized by madness and sexual panic even though it is a moment that is important in recognizing serious abuses that deserve to be called out.

Bartholet argued that when the posture of Democratic senators is examined

cynically, I just wonder how much credibility it has with Democrats openly talking about the need to do this so they could be in the superior position to the Republicans.

In a phone interview, Bartholet noted the danger

in going too far in limiting relational autonomy. Where do people meet other people? Largely in college, graduate school and work. You do not want to go too far in making relationships in these contexts dangerous.

Since hierarchical relationships are pervasive in these environments, Bartholet argues, there is a need also

to distinguish between sexual/romantic advances made by men in power and real abuses of power.

Bartholet has been one of the leading critics of the sexual harassment policies now adopted by Harvard and many other colleges and universities. In October 2014, she and 27 other members of the Harvard Law School faculty published a letter in the Boston Globe that challenged the university's harassment policy on a wide range of points. Some of those points are relevant to the current national debate over Franken and other accused politicians:

The goal must not be simply to go as far as possible in the direction of preventing anything that some might characterize as sexual harassment. The goal must instead be to fully address sexual harassment while at the same time protecting students against unfair and inappropriate discipline, honoring individual relationship autonomy, and maintaining the values of academic freedom. The law that the Supreme Court and lower federal courts have developed under Title IX and Title VII attempts to balance all these important interests. The university's sexual harassment policy departs dramatically from these legal principles, jettisoning balance and fairness in the rush to appease certain federal administrative officials.

With both political parties coming to realize that the issue of sexual harassment and misconduct may determine who is inaugurated on Jan. 20, 2021, the goal of "balanced" interests will be superseded, at least temporarily, by exigent political considerations.

As Slate noted earlier this year, the Zervos defamation lawsuit "is daring Trump to incriminate himself in court" and to fall into the same perjury trap Bill Clinton did in the Paula Jones case — perjury which led to Clinton's impeachment. And if Democrats retake either the House or the Senate in 2018, it is a virtual certainty that Trump's accusers will be called to provide sworn testimony, and that the perjury trap will loom again if and when Trump is offered the opportunity to rebut them under oath.

Democrats go into 2018 with the deck stacked against them — in the House by a combination of gerrymandering and the concentration of Democratic voters in relatively few districts and in the Senate, by the fact that 23 Democratic seats are up, along with those of the 2 independents who caucus with the Democrats, compared to only 8 Republican seats. Ten of the Democratic seats are in states carried by Trump.

Insofar as sexual harassment and misconduct become an electoral issue, it will help the Democrats, but the party cannot depend on that alone to produce a change in control of either branch of Congress. No one knows what the half life of this issue is. Although right now it seems unlikely, it could once again become nearly as invisible as it was three months ago. At the moment, the Democrats' best ally in building the momentum necessary for a power shift is Trump himself, who has been doing all he can to create the next Democratic wave.

Microsoft Moves to End Secrecy in Sexual Harassment Claims

BY NICK WINGFIELD AND JESSICA SILVER-GREENBERG | DEC. 19, 2017

SEATTLE — The wave of sexual harassment claims has toppled powerful men in entertainment, media and politics. Now, it is also creating permanent changes in workplace policy at one giant technology company.

Microsoft, one of the world's biggest software makers, said on Tuesday that it had eliminated forced arbitration agreements with employees who make sexual harassment claims and was also supporting a proposed federal law that would widely ban such agreements.

The moves make Microsoft an early company — and certainly the most prominent — to take such steps to end legal agreements that have been criticized for helping to perpetuate sexual abuse in the workplace. Forced arbitration lets companies keep harassment and discrimination claims out of court, effectively cloaking them from public view and, in some cases, allowing serial harassers to continue their conduct for years.

"The silencing of people's voices has clearly had an impact in perpetuating sexual harassment," Brad Smith, Microsoft's president and chief legal officer, said in a phone interview.

Microsoft's action shows how the flood of harassment accusations has gone beyond individual cases to an examination of policy changes for ending the misconduct. That includes greater scrutiny of legal settlements that have silenced victims of abuse.

In one prominent case, an arbitration clause nearly prevented Gretchen Carlson, the former Fox News anchor, from bringing her lawsuit over sexual harassment against Roger Ailes, the former chairman and chief executive of Fox News. Ms. Carlson found a legal maneuver allowing her into court, but many employees are not as lucky.

In an op-ed article in The New York Times in October, Ms. Carlson wrote that "reforming arbitration laws is key to stopping sexual harassment." According to the Economic Policy Institute, more than half of American workers are bound by arbitration clauses.

Since then, lawmakers have taken up the issue. This month, a bipartisan group of senators, including Lindsey Graham, Republican of South Carolina, and Kirsten Gillibrand, Democrat of New York, proposed legislation that would make forced arbitration in harassment cases unenforceable under federal law.

Mr. Smith of Microsoft said he first became aware of the Senate bill after meeting with Mr. Graham in Washington to discuss cybersecurity and immigration. Mr. Graham urged Microsoft to support the bill, Mr. Smith said.

"What this legislation does is ensure that peoples' voices can always be heard by going to court, if that's what it takes for those voices to be heard," Mr. Smith said. "It's the kind of step that can make a difference."

He said eliminating the arbitration requirement for harassment claims by its own employees represented an immediate step the company could take while the Senate bill was being considered. The move is largely symbolic because only a minority of Microsoft workers — numbering in the hundreds in its senior ranks, according to Mr. Smith — have been subject to the requirement. Microsoft will still require those employees to take claims unrelated to harassment and gender discrimination to arbitration. In total, Microsoft has about 125,000 employees around the world.

Like other technology companies, Microsoft has faced accusations that it has tolerated harassment and discrimination against female employees. Last week, Bloomberg reported that documents unsealed in a gender bias case showed that an unnamed former intern for Microsoft accused another intern of sexually assaulting her outside of work, and that Microsoft required the two of them to continue working together while it investigated the claims.

In a statement, Microsoft said it did not tolerate sexual harassment or assault. "We work hard to create a safe work environment for every employee," the company said, adding that it encouraged the former intern to take her complaint to law enforcement.

Ms. Gillibrand said that getting rid of the arbitration agreements would benefit employers in the long run. "Without the secrecy of mandatory arbitration agreements, serial predators will be less likely to continue climbing the corporate ladder and employees won't be forced to stay quiet about the harassment they have faced at work, which is good for employees and good for business," she said in a statement.

By using the arbitration clauses to bar people from joining together as a group, employers — both large and small — have effectively taken away one of the few tools that workers have to fight harassment or discrimination.

The Equal Employment Opportunity Commission has found that forced arbitration "can prevent employees from learning about similar concerns shared by others in their workplace." Given the proliferation of the clauses, some regulators and civil rights experts also worry that arbitration clauses can obscure patterns of wrongdoing.

Strict confidentiality can turn up in a variety of contexts, from payday-lending outfits, which sometimes rely on them to conceal the true identity of lenders that operate through shell companies, to personal relationships. Employment contracts are among the most problematic, lawyers said.

In arbitration, the rules tilt heavily in favor of businesses, employment experts said. Part of the problem is that instead of judges, cases are decided by arbitrators who sometimes consider the companies that routinely bring them business their clients, according to interviews with arbitrators.

The more often companies head to arbitration, the better their chances of winning the case, according to the conclusion of a 2011 analysis by Alexander J. S. Colvin, a professor at Cornell University's School of Industrial and Labor Relations.

Of 3,945 employment cases decided by arbitrators from one of the nation's biggest arbitration firms, plaintiffs prevailed in about 31 percent of them when employers had only one case before the arbitrator, according to Mr. Colvin's study. The rate of victory for employees plummeted by more than half when companies had multiple cases before the same arbitrator.

NICK WINGFIELD REPORTED FROM SEATTLE, AND JESSICA SILVER-GREENBERG FROM NEW YORK.

Business Schools Now Teaching #MeToo, N.F.L. Protests and Trump

BY DAVID GELLES AND CLAIRE CAIN MILLER | DEC. 25, 2017

NASHVILLE — Tim Vogus, a professor at Vanderbilt University's business school, was stoking the debate in his classroom one day this fall, asking first-year M.B.A. students about one of the most successful, and controversial, companies of the day. On the syllabus was Uber, a case study in both sensational business success and rampant corporate misbehavior.

"A toxic culture might be obvious when you think about Uber," Professor Vogus said. "But I'm an old person. What is this whole 'bro' thing?"

There were some awkward chuckles, and then hands started popping up. "It's carrying fraternity culture with you into adult life," said one student, Nick Glennon. Another student, Jonathon Brangan, said, "It's arrogance mixed with the feeling of invincibility."

CHRIS PHILPOT

Alex Parr, a student in Prof. Ed Soule's class at Georgetown's McDonough School of Business, discussing protests by N.F.L. players.

"You basically have these 20-year-olds who are in charge of these companies that are worth billions of dollars," said Monroe Stadler, 26. "And they fly too close to the sun."

An M.B.A. education is no longer just about finance, marketing, accounting and economics. As topics like sexual harassment dominate the national conversation and chief executives weigh in on the ethical and social issues of the day, business schools around the country are hastily reshaping their curriculums with case studies ripped straight from the headlines.

At Vanderbilt, there are classes on Uber and "bro" culture. At Stanford, students are studying sexual harassment in the workplace. And at Harvard, the debate encompasses sexism and free speech.

"There's a turning point in what's expected from business leaders," said Leanne Meyer, co-director of a new leadership department at the Carnegie Mellon Tepper School of Business. "Up until now, business leaders were largely responsible for delivering products. Now, shareholders are looking to corporate leaders to make statements on what would traditionally have been social justice or moral issues."

Several factors are contributing to these revised syllabuses. Bad behavior by big companies has thrust ethics back into the news, from Wells Fargo's creation of fake accounts to sexual harassment at Fox News to the litany of improprieties at Uber. Some millennials are prioritizing social and environmental responsibility.

And a new generation of chief executives is speaking out about moral and political issues in the Trump era. Just four months ago, prominent corporate executives came together to dissolve two business councils consulting with President Trump after he blamed "many sides" for an outburst of white supremacist violence in Charlottesville, Va.

"Something has changed," said Ed Soule, a professor at the Georgetown McDonough School of Business. "I would be kidding you if I told you there wasn't a different vibe in the classroom."

This fall, Professor Soule assigned coursework covering sexual harassment at Uber, how companies like Amazon respond when attacked by Mr. Trump and the social justice protests by N.F.L. players.

During one class, students debated whether players should have been more deferential to the wishes of team owners and the league, or whether the league should have supported players more vocally. The conversation grew tense when the topic turned to respect for the national anthem, and Mr. Trump's forceful response to players who continued to kneel as it was played.

"Ethics and values have taken on more significance," Professor Soule said. "It has to do with all of the things going on in this administration, often things that challenge our understanding of ethicsand leadership."

Professors are reacting to the news, but they are also responding to calls from students for classes that deal with ethics. In recent years, students have said ethical issues, not finances, are a business's most important responsibility, according to a survey of business school students worldwide conducted by a United Nations group and Macquarie University in Australia.

"There's a growing body of M.B.A.s who are really passionate about this," said LaToya Marc, who graduated from Harvard Business School last spring and now works in sales and operations at Comcast. "It may not affect your bottom line directly, but it needs to be affecting how you make decisions."

Students also realize that as leaders of increasingly diverse work forces, they will need to understand their employees' perspectives on national debates, and how corporate decisions affect them.

"It is a shift, absolutely, mostly because all of our companies are just starting to look a lot different," Ms. Marc said.

One way that some business schools are responding is by drawing on the social sciences, like behavioral economics and psychology. The Stanford Graduate School of Business's ethics class — taught by two political scientists, one an expert in behavior and the other in game theory — sounds more like a course in human nature than in finance.

A new topic this year is sexual harassment, and how to create a workplace culture in which people feel comfortable reporting it. The Stanford students studied psychological research showing that people are more willing to challenge authority if at least one other person joins them, and discussed ways to encourage such reporting.

Next year, Fern Mandelbaum, a venture capitalist, will teach a new class to Stanford M.B.A. candidates called Equity by Design: Building Diverse and Inclusive Organizations.

"It's not just how the C.E.O. of Uber was treating women," Ms. Mandelbaum said. "The bias is throughout the system."

Carnegie Mellon started its leadership department after hearing from alumni that it needed more training related to skills like empathy and communication. This fall, Ms. Meyer's students studied a contentious memo written by a Google engineer, who was then fired, arguing that women were less suited to engineering than men.

"We said, 'This is not just a gender issue. It's a business issue,'" Ms. Meyer said. "It has marketing implications, legal implications, H.R. implications."

Gender is an issue that students are particularly interested in, according to the Forté Foundation, which works with business schools to help more women advance into leadership roles. The foundation has developed a tool kit for men, with tips like choosing a name such as "ally" or "liaison" to denote a sense of partnership, or using role-playing scenarios about sensitive situations, like what to do if a colleague says, "She only got the promotion because she's a woman."

Two dozen schools have started groups based on the program, including groups called the Manbassadors, for men committed to gender equity in business, at the business schools at Columbia, Dartmouth and Harvard.

The goal is "making sure that as men we're very aware of some of the privileges we're afforded simply because of gender," said Alen Amini, a third-year student at the Tuck School of Business at Dartmouth and a founder of its Manbassadors group.

JUSTIN T. GELLERSON FOR THE NEW YORK TIMES

"Something has changed," Professor Soule said. "I would be kidding you if I told you there wasn't a different vibe in the classroom."

As previously taboo subjects enter the classroom debate, students and professors are still adjusting.

"It can get pretty controversial," said Aaron Chatterji, an associate professor at the Duke University Fuqua School of Business who is starting a class about activism among chief executives. "I've never taught a class where I've had students talking about gay rights or drug addiction."

At Vanderbilt, Professor Vogus solicited ideas from the class about how Uber might change its ways. One student suggested hiring fewer star engineers and more team players. Another proposed hiring a woman to lead human resources.

"We have a 'C.E.-bro' culture in the technology sector today, but we've had 'C.E.-bros' throughout time," said a student, April Hughes. "Enron was an example of this. All the guys there thought they were smarter than everyone else."

The class turned testy, however, as students debated whether Uber's hard-charging culture might have been an asset.

"Some of that brashness was actually critical to the company being successful," said one student, Andrew Bininger.

When the Uber conversation turned to gender and power dynamics, a female student suggested that women in the Vanderbilt M.B.A. program had to work harder than their male counterparts.

"The women who do make it to business school are all super strong personalities, whereas the men here can float through without being the cream of the crop," Natalie Copley said, adding of the women in the class, "They're not meek little timid things."

That drew jeers from the men in the group, and Professor Vogus changed the subject.

The Patriarchs Are Falling.
The Patriarchy Is Stronger Than Ever.

OPINION | BY SUSAN FALUDI | DEC. 28, 2017

IT WOULD BE EASY to end 2017 with the impression that, whatever its afflictions, it was at least a game-changing year for feminism.

"The Female Revolution Is Here" and could "Smash Patriarchy at Its Core," social and mainstream media headlines declared. "We are blowing the whistle on the prime directive of the master/slave relationship between women and men." "This is the end of patriarchy" — this from Forbes! — "the male domination of humanity." Twitter, the newsstand and the street concur: This year witnessed a transformational moment in American sexual politics.

Surely the results of the #MeToo phenomenon are worthy. It's a seriously good thing Harvey Weinstein is gone and that the potential Harvey Weinsteins will think twice or thrice or a thousand times before harassing women whose fortunes they control. But "the end of patriarchy"? Look around.

This month, President Trump signed into law a tax bill that throws a bomb at women. The Tax Cuts and Jobs Act systematically guts benefits that support women who need support the most: It means an end to personal and dependent exemptions (a disaster for minimum-wage workers, nearly two-thirds of whom are women). An expiration date for child-care tax credits and a denial of such credits for immigrant children without Social Security cards. An end to the Affordable Care Act's individual mandate. And, barely avoided, thanks to Democrats' objections: an enshrinement of "fetal personhood" in the form of college savings accounts for unborn children, a sly grenade lobbed at legal abortion.

Not to mention that Republican congressmen plan to pay down the enormous federal deficit the bill will incur by slashing entitlements that, again, are critical to women: Medicaid (covering nearly half the births in the nation and 75 percent of family planning), Medicare (more than half of beneficiaries 65 and older — and two-thirds of those 85 and older — are women) and so on.

And that's on top of all the other Trump administration insults: reviving the global gag rule on abortion, suspending tracking of the gender wage gap, deep-sixing the Fair Pay and Safe Workplaces executive order and much more.

Which leads me to wonder, if we get rid of a handful of Harveys while losing essential rights and protections for millions of women, are we really winning this thing? How is this female calamity happening in the midst of the Female Revolution? An answer may lie in a schism that has haunted women's protest for 150 years.

American women's activism has historically taken two forms. One is an expression of direct anger at the ways individual men use and abuse us. It's righteous outrage against the unambiguous enemy with a visible face, the male predator who feeds on our vulnerability and relishes our humiliation. Mr. Weinstein's face is the devil's face du jour, and the #MeToo campaign fits squarely in this camp. The other form is less spectacular but as essential: It's fighting the ways the world is structurally engineered against women. Tied to that fight is the difficult and ambiguous labor of building an equitable system within which women have the wherewithal and power to lead full lives.

The clarion cry against individual male predation and the push for broader gender equality may seem part and parcel, especially now. When Donald Trump is the titular head of the machine, it's tempting to imagine that the machine itself has orange hair — and that to defeat Harvey Weinstein is to win. But the patriarchy is bigger than the patriarch.

The two forms of women's protest intersect, of course. Just ask generations of female workers at Ford Motor Company, who know that workplace sexual harassment undergirds a system of oppression. But fighting the patriarch and fighting the patriarchy are also distinct — and the former tends to be more popular than the latter. It's easier to mobilize against a demon, as every military propagandist — and populist demagogue — knows. It's harder, and less electrifying, to forge the terms of peace. Declaring war is thrilling. Nation building isn't.

How this plays out in feminism has been evident since the 19th century, when American women started the "social purity" movement against prostitution and "white slavery" of girls. The most popular women's mobilization of the 19th century wasn't for suffrage — it was for Prohibition, a moral crusade against demon men drinking demon rum, blowing their paychecks at the saloon and coming home to beat and rape their wives. The Women's Christian Temperance Union quickly became the nation's largest women's organization.

Did that war against men behaving badly feed into the larger battle for women's equality? In many ways, yes: Susan B. Anthony herself began as a temperance organizer. But a good number of women who railed against alcohol's evils shrank from women's suffrage. Fighting against male drunkenness fell within the time-honored female purview of defending the family and the body; extending women's rights into a new political realm felt more radical and less immediate. Frances Willard, the temperance union's formidable second president, eventually brought the organization around to supporting the female franchise by redefining the women's vote as a "home protection" issue: "citizen mothers," as the morally superior sex, would purge social degeneracy from the domestic and public circle. But Willard's attempt to further conjoin morality efforts with the second form of activism — her "Do Everything" campaign for a shorter workweek, a living wage, health care and prison reform, among other things — was snuffed out upon her death, as the union's leadership abandoned its support for broader social reform.

The challenge today is the one faced by Anthony and Willard: how to bring the outrage over male malfeasance to bear on the more far-reaching campaign for women's equality. Too often, the world's attention seems to have room for only the first.

A few weeks ago on a chilly morning in Pittsburgh, two women named Chelsey Engel and Lindsey Disler chained themselves to the entrance of the building that houses Senator Pat Toomey's local office to protest the tax bill. "The situation is so catastrophic and so dire," Ms. Disler said, her scarf-swathed torso shackled to the doors. "Something has to be done." She delivered her words to two dozen onlookers and a few police officers, who, by 8:30 a.m., had sent the two women packing. Their protest barely registered outside a few area news outlets, on a day when the media was aflutter with reports of the latest celebrity accused of harassment, Peter Martins, director of New York City Ballet.

The two forms of female protest can even be positioned against each other. In the 1980s, the "War on Pornography" campaign set off the damaging "sex wars" within the women's movement itself, at the very moment when a backlash against women's equality was amassing its forces and Ronald Reagan's administration was formulating policies that would disproportionately hurt half the country. The "sex-positive" feminists who worried about restrictions on free speech and questioned the condemnation of all pornographic material found themselves labeled, by anti-pornography feminists, as shills and pimps for the industry. Today we're already seeing the long knives come out for sister travelers who have called for some due process and proportionality in confronting male harassers.

A similar quarrel surfaced in Hillary Clinton's defeat last year. Some feminist-minded women deemed her an unacceptable choice to pursue the art of dealing and compromising necessary to running the state — and running it to the greater benefit of women — because she'd already compromised herself by staying with, and defending, Bill Clinton.

The forces behind this divide are so intractable in part because they are so psychological. To fight the devil is to be on the side of the angels, to assume the mantle of virtue and purity. The political arena, by contrast, is no place for angels, and its victories are slow and often incomplete. Without gainsaying the courage of "silence breakers," one can note the flip side: that their words, especially now, can generate instant, and dramatic, response — and more immediate gratification than one gets from protesting economic and legal structures.

Since Mr. Trump's election, women have been trying hard to fight on both fronts. The #MeToo campaign exists alongside the Women's March on Washington, black female voters sending an Alabama Democrat to the Senate, and a stunning number of female candidates seeking office in coming elections. If women can break the hex that has kept them from harnessing the pure politics of personal outrage to the impure politics of society building, then maybe our Chelsey Engels and Lindsey Dislers can draw as much attention to their protest as the next actress will outing the next loathsome boss.

That paradigm shift will be critical to winning the coming battles for women's rights: health insurance, pay equity, family planning, sexual assault, and more. The peril is that activist women won't transcend the divide. In which case, #MeToo will continue to topple patriarchs, while the patriarchy continues to win the day.

Powerful Hollywood Women Unveil Anti-Harassment Action Plan

BY CARA BUCKLEY | JAN. 1, 2018

DRIVEN BY OUTRAGE and a resolve to correct a power imbalance that seemed intractable just months ago, 300 prominent actresses and female agents, writers, directors, producers and entertainment executives have formed an ambitious, sprawling initiative to fight systemic sexual harassment in Hollywood and in blue-collar workplaces nationwide.

The initiative includes:

• A legal defense fund, backed by $13 million in donations, to help less privileged women — like janitors, nurses and workers at farms, factories, restaurants and hotels — protect themselves from sexual misconduct and the fallout from reporting it.

CLOCKWISE FROM TOP LEFT: FIRST TWO PHOTOS, BRINSON+BANKS FOR THE NEW YORK TIMES; ORIANA KOREN FOR THE NEW YORK TIMES; BRINSON+BANKS FOR THE NEW YORK TIMES.

Some of the women who established Time's Up, clockwise from top left: actresses America Ferrera and Eva Longoria; lawyer Nina L. Shaw; and producer Shonda Rhimes.

• Legislation to penalize companies that tolerate persistent harassment, and to discourage the use of nondisclosure agreements to silence victims.

• A drive to reach gender parity at studios and talent agencies that has already begun making headway.

• And a request that women walking the red carpet at the Golden Globes speak out and raise awareness by wearing black.

Called Time's Up, the movement was announced on Monday with an impassioned pledge of support to working-class women in an open letter signed by hundreds of women in show business, many of them A-listers. The letter also ran as a full-page ad in The New York Times, and in La Opinion, a Spanish-language newspaper.

"The struggle for women to break in, to rise up the ranks and to simply be heard and acknowledged in male-dominated workplaces must end; time's up on this impenetrable monopoly," the letter says.

The group is one answer to the question of how women in Hollywood would respond to cascading allegations that have upended the careers of powerful men in an industry where the prevalence of sexual predation has yielded the minimizing cliché of the "casting couch," and where silence has been a condition of employment.

Time's Up also helps defuse criticism that the spotlight on the #MeToo movement has been dominated by the accusers of high-profile men, while the travails of working-class women have been overlooked.

This was highlighted in November, when an open letter was sent on behalf of 700,000 female farmworkers who said they stood with Hollywood actresses in their fight against abuse. Time's Up members said the letter bolstered their resolve to train their efforts on both Hollywood and beyond.

"It's very hard for us to speak righteously about the rest of anything if we haven't cleaned our own house," said Shonda Rhimes, the executive producer of the television series "Grey's Anatomy," "Scandal" and "How to Get Away With Murder," who has been closely involved with the group.

"If this group of women can't fight for a model for other women who don't have as much power and privilege, then who can?" Ms. Rhimes continued.

Other Time's Up members include the actresses Ashley Judd, Eva Longoria, America Ferrera, Natalie Portman, Rashida Jones, Emma Stone, Kerry Washington and Reese Witherspoon; the showrunner Jill Soloway; Donna Langley, chairwoman of Universal Pictures; the lawyers Nina L. Shaw and Tina Tchen, who served as Michelle Obama's chief of staff; and Maria Eitel, an expert in corporate responsibility who is co-chairwoman of the Nike Foundation.

"People were moved so viscerally," said Ms. Eitel, who helps moderate Time's Up meetings, which began in October. "They didn't come together because they wanted to whine, or complain, or tell a story or bemoan. They came together because they intended to act. There was almost a ferociousness to it, especially in the first meetings."

Time's Up is leaderless, run by volunteers and made up of working groups. One group oversaw the creation of a commission, led by Anita Hill and announced in December, that is tasked with creating a blueprint for ending sexual harassment in show business.

Another group, 50/50by2020, is pushing entertainment organizations and companies to agree to reach gender parity in their leadership tiers within two years. It already can claim a victory. In early December, after Ms. Rhimes pressed him, Chris Silbermann, a managing director at ICM Partners, pledged that his talent agency would meet that goal.

"We just reached this conclusion in our heads that, damn it, everything is possible," Ms. Rhimes said. "Why shouldn't it be?"

There is also a group ensuring that minorities and gays, lesbians, bisexuals and transgender people are heard. "No one wants to look back and say they stood at the sidelines," said Lena Waithe, a star of the Netflix series "Master of None" and part of that working group.

Another group is devising legislation to tackle abuses and address how nondisclosure agreements silence victims of sexual harassment.

"People settling out in advance of their rights is obviously something that can't continue," said Ms. Shaw, a prominent lawyer whose clients have included Lupita Nyong'o and Ava DuVernay.

Ms. Tchen is spearheading the Time's Up Legal Defense Fund, which is administered by the National Women's Law Center's Legal Network for Gender Equity, and will connect female victims of sexual harassment with lawyers. Major donors include Ms. Witherspoon, Ms. Rhimes, Meryl Streep, Steven Spielberg and Kate Capshaw, and the talent agencies ICM Partners, the Creative Artists Agency, William Morris Endeavor and United Talent Agency.

Time's Up has also been urging women to wear black at the Golden Globes on Sunday, to use the red carpet to speak out against gender and racial inequality, and to raise awareness about their initiative and the legal fund.

"This is a moment of solidarity, not a fashion moment," Ms. Longoria said. A vast majority of the women who had been contacted and planned to attend the ceremony pledged to participate, she said.

"For years, we've sold these awards shows as women, with our gowns and colors and our beautiful faces and our glamour," Ms. Longoria said. "This time the industry can't expect us to go up and twirl around. That's not what this moment is about."

Time's Up was formed soon after The New York Times reported in early October that the producer Harvey Weinstein had reached multiple settlements with women who had accused him of sexual misconduct.

As more women stepped forward, and more men were accused of abuse, a group of female talent agents met at Creative Artists to discuss the problem and explore solutions. The group soon expanded to dozens and, eventually, about 150 participants (it has since doubled as the actresses who joined expanded to New York and London), who meet weekly at the agency and in living rooms across Los Angeles, as well as for daylong workshops.

Katie McGrath, who runs the production company Bad Robot with her husband, J. J. Abrams (both are also major donors to the legal fund), said that the women realized from the start that they needed to figure out "what we wanted out of this moment, and what was going to be required in order to shift and pivot from this horror to structural change."

Several of the women said their work with Time's Up presented a rare opportunity to meet regularly and pool efforts with other powerful women. In an industry overwhelmingly dominated by men, they said, they were usually one of the few actresses on set, or one of the few female writers or producers in a room.

"We have been siloed off from each other," Ms. Witherspoon said. "We're finally hearing each other, and seeing each other, and now locking arms in solidarity with each other, and in solidarity for every woman who doesn't feel seen, to be finally heard."

No one can predict whether this burst of energy will lead to lasting changes. Time's Up members said the meetings had brought disagreements and frustrations as well. "It's not as satisfying as finding a silver bullet," Ms. Ferrera said. "We all recognize there's no such thing." But, she added, "not taking action is no longer an option."

Ms. Rhimes said working with the group of women reminded her of a feeling she got as a child, when her mother took her around the neighborhood in a wagon to register black women to vote. "We're a bunch of women used to getting stuff done," she said. "And we're getting stuff done."

#MeToo Has Done
What the Law Could Not

OPINION | BY CATHARINE A. MACKINNON | FEB. 4, 2018

THE #METOO MOVEMENT is accomplishing what sexual harassment law to date has not.

This mass mobilization against sexual abuse, through an unprecedented wave of speaking out in conventional and social media, is eroding the two biggest barriers to ending sexual harassment in law and in life: the disbelief and trivializing dehumanization of its victims.

Sexual harassment law — the first law to conceive sexual violation in inequality terms — created the preconditions for this moment. Yet denial by abusers and devaluing of accusers could still be reasonably counted on by perpetrators to shield their actions.

GABRIELLA DEMCZUK FOR THE NEW YORK TIMES

Democratic House members dressed in black on Tuesday in a show of solidarity against sexual assault.

Many survivors realistically judged reporting pointless. Complaints were routinely passed off with some version of "she wasn't credible" or "she wanted it." I kept track of this in cases of campus sexual abuse over decades; it typically took three to four women testifying that they had been violated by the same man in the same way to even begin to make a dent in his denial. That made a woman, for credibility purposes, one-fourth of a person.

Even when she was believed, nothing he did to her mattered as much as what would be done to him if his actions against her were taken seriously. His value outweighed her sexualized worthlessness. His career, reputation, mental and emotional serenity and assets counted. Hers didn't. In some ways, it was even worse to be believed and not have what he did matter. It meant she didn't matter.

These dynamics of inequality have preserved the system in which the more power a man has, the more sexual access he can get away with compelling.

It is widely thought that when something is legally prohibited, it more or less stops. This may be true for exceptional acts, but it is not true for pervasive practices like sexual harassment, including rape, that are built into structural social hierarchies. Equal pay has been the law for decades and still does not exist. Racial discrimination is nominally illegal in many forms but is still widely practiced against people of color. If the same cultural inequalities are permitted to operate in law as in the behavior the law prohibits, equalizing attempts — such as sexual harassment law — will be systemically resisted.

This logjam, which has long paralyzed effective legal recourse for sexual harassment, is finally being broken. Structural misogyny, along with sexualized racism and class inequalities, is being publicly and pervasively challenged by women's voices. The difference is, power is paying attention.

Powerful individuals and entities are taking sexual abuse seriously for once and acting against it as never before. No longer liars, no longer worthless, today's survivors are initiating consequences none of them could have gotten through any lawsuit — in part because the laws do not permit relief against individual perpetrators, but more because they are being believed and valued as the law seldom has. Women have been saying these things forever. It is the response to them that has changed.

Revulsion against harassing behavior — in this case, men with power refusing to be associated with it — could change workplaces and schools. It could restrain repeat predators as well as the occasional and casual exploiters that the law so far has not. Shunning perpetrators as sex bigots who take advantage of the vulnerabilities of inequality could transform society. It could change rape culture.

Sexual harassment law can grow with #MeToo. Taking #MeToo's changing norms into the law could — and predictably will — transform the law as well. Some practical steps could help capture this moment. Institutional or statutory changes could include prohibitions or limits on various forms of secrecy and nontransparency that hide the extent of sexual abuse and enforce survivor isolation, such as forced arbitration, silencing nondisclosure agreements even in cases of physical attacks and multiple perpetration, and confidential settlements. A realistic statute of limitations for all forms of discrimination, including sexual harassment, is essential. Being able to sue individual perpetrators and their enablers, jointly with institutions, could shift perceived incentives for this behavior. The only legal change that matches the scale of this moment is an Equal Rights Amendment, expanding the congressional power to legislate against sexual abuse and judicial interpretations of existing law, guaranteeing equality under the Constitution for all.

But it is #MeToo, this uprising of the formerly disregarded, that has made untenable the assumption that the one who reports sexual abuse is a lying slut, and that is changing everything already. Sexual harassment law prepared the ground, but it is today's movement that is shifting gender hierarchy's tectonic plates.

CHAPTER 4

Criticism of the #MeToo Movement

Accusations of sexual assault in a #MeToo world often result in swift, unchallenged punishment. Some people, such as French actress Catherine Deneuve, Canadian novelist Margaret Atwood, and American actor Matt Damon, encouraged the public to consider the source, context, and nature of the allegations. Others cautioned against vigilante justice and ignoring the rights of the accused. And some pointed out that the reactive, uninhibited nature of social media posts could undermine the potential for long-term change presented by the #MeToo movement.

Matt Damon Draws Rebukes for Comments on the #MeToo Movement

BY CHRISTINA CARON | DEC. 17, 2017

THE ACTOR MATT DAMON waded into the national conversation about sexual assault in an interview with ABC News on Thursday, observing that men are being lumped into "one big bucket" when in reality there is a "spectrum of behavior."

"There's a difference between, you know, patting someone on the butt and rape or child molestation, right?" he told Peter Travers of ABC. "Both of those behaviors need to be confronted and eradicated without question, but they shouldn't be conflated, right?"

Those comments were met with anger and frustration online, where many women, including the actress Alyssa Milano, rejected attempts to categorize various forms of sexual misconduct.

"They all hurt," Ms. Milano wrote on Twitter on Friday. "And they are all connected to a patriarchy intertwined with normalized, accepted — even welcomed — misogyny."

Other critiques soon followed — with some women speaking up in Mr. Damon's defense — but the tenor of the conversation was the same: frustration, anger and exasperation.

That groundswell of testimony that has empowered women to speak publicly about sexual harassment and abuse is posing challenges about how best to have a national conversation about a subject that previously lingered in the shadows.

"The #MeToo movement has exposed that we don't have a shared, fully developed, robust way of talking about everyday violence — especially sexual violence in the lives of women," Leigh Gilmore, a visiting professor in women's and gender studies at Wellesley College in Wellesley, Mass., and author of "Tainted Witness: Why We Doubt What Women Say About Their Lives," said in a phone interview on Sunday. "We just don't have a ready vocabulary for it."

Mr. Damon said the #MeToo movement had been eye-opening for him.

"I think one of the surprising things for me has been the extent to which my female friends, as, I think, of all the ones I've talked to in the last year since all this stuff started happening — I can't think of any of them who don't have a story at some point in their life," he said in the interview. "And most of them have more than one."

He's not alone in that sentiment. The volume of revelations about sexual harassment and assault has been overwhelming at times.

"It's the same world, but the coordinates feel really different," Ms. Gilmore said. "In this moment, everything feels upside down."

In the wide-ranging 16-minute interview, Mr. Damon discussed Harvey Weinstein ("Nobody who made movies for him knew"), confidential settlements ("The day of the confidentiality agreements is over") and raising four daughters in the era of #MeToo ("You just have to raise children with, like, self-esteem, because you're not going to be there to make all of their decisions for them").

But it was his comment about the current "culture of outrage and injury" that inflamed passions online.

"None of us came here perfect," he said. "What's the point of us being here other than to improve?"

Ms. Milano responded: "We are in a 'culture of outrage' because the magnitude of rage is, in fact, overtly outrageous. And it is righteous."

Minnie Driver, who once dated Mr. Damon and starred with him in the 1997 film "Good Will Hunting," also expressed disbelief on Twitter.

In an interview with The Guardian on Saturday, Ms. Driver said men "simply cannot understand what abuse is like on a daily level."

"I honestly think that until we get on the same page, you can't tell a woman about their abuse," she said. "A man cannot do that. No one can. It is so individual and so personal, it's galling when a powerful man steps up and starts dictating the terms, whether he intends it or not."

When #MeToo Goes Too Far

OPINION | BY BRET STEPHENS | DEC. 20, 2017

MATT DAMON gave an interview to ABC News last week in which he offered the following observation: "There's a difference between, you know, patting someone on the butt and rape or child molestation, right? Both of those behaviors need to be confronted and eradicated without question, but they shouldn't be conflated, right?"

Crazy, right?

Minnie Driver, Damon's co-star in "Good Will Hunting," thought so. "There is no hierarchy of abuse — that if a woman is raped [it] is much worse than if a woman has a penis exposed to her that she didn't want or ask for," she told The Guardian. "You cannot tell those women that one is supposed to feel worse than the other."

Kirsten Gillibrand agrees: "I think when we start having to talk about the differences between sexual assault and sexual harassment and unwanted groping, you are having the wrong conversation," the Democratic senator from New York said at a news conference when asked about calling on Senator Al Franken to resign. "You need to draw a line in the sand and say none of it is O.K. None of it is acceptable."

Of course none of it is O.K. The supposedly petty sexual harassment that so many women have to endure, from Hollywood studios to the factory floor at Ford, is a national outrage that needs to end. Period.

But what about the idea that we should not even discuss the difference between verbal harassment, physical groping and rape? Here's a guess: A vast majority of Americans, men and women, would agree with Damon's comment in its entirety.

Another guess: A majority of women would not accept Driver's suggestion that the unwanted sight of a man's genitals, as wrong as it is, is anywhere near as traumatic as the unspeakably violent experience of rape.

Think of it a moment more. If, as Driver put it, "there is no hierarchy of abuse," then should Harvey Weinstein and Al Franken be punished in the same way? Should George H. W. Bush be subjected to the same obloquy as Louis C.K.?

All societies make necessary moral distinctions between high crimes and misdemeanors, mortal and lesser sins. A murderer is worse than a thief. A drug dealer is worse than a user. And so on. Gillibrand, Driver and others want to blur such distinctions, on the theory that we need a zero-tolerance approach. That may sound admirable, but it's legally unworkable and, in many cases, simply unjust.

It's also destructive, above all to the credibility of the #MeToo movement. Social movements rarely succeed if they violate our gut sense of decency and moral proportion. Insofar as #MeToo has made an example of a Harvey Weinstein or a Matt Lauer, most Americans — including, I'd bet, most men — have been on its side.

But what about a case such as Glenn Thrush, The Times's reporter who was suspended after being accused of inappropriate sexual behavior and, The Times said Wednesday, will keep his job but not his White House beat? Or what about Stephen Henderson, the Pulitzer Prize-winning Detroit Free Press columnist and editorial page editor (and an acquaintance of mine) who was recently sacked from his job?

Henderson is not accused of sexual assault. He is widely admired as a pillar and champion of his hometown. And Henderson has apologized for his behavior, which he said happened years ago and involved "sexually themed conversations" with a co-worker outside of work along with a couple of rejected passes at a woman working in another department.

Does this behavior really merit professional decapitation? Wouldn't the apology, plus, say, a monthlong suspension, have sufficed? Don't we have the moral capacity to distinguish between aggressive sexual predation and run-of-the-mill romantic bungling — between a pattern of abusive behavior and a good man's uncharacteristic bad moments? And do companies really have the resources, or the right, to police and adjudicate the private behavior of their employees?

It will not serve the interests of women if #MeToo becomes a movement that does as much to wreck the careers of people like Henderson as it does to bring down the Weinsteins of the world. Nor will it do much to convince men that #MeToo is a movement that is ultimately for them if every sexual transgression, great or small, vile, crass or mostly clumsy, is judged according to the same Procrustean standard.

Now to the inevitable rejoinder: You're a guy. What do you know? Or, as Minnie Driver told The Guardian: "The time right now is for men just to listen and not have an opinion about it for once."

Listening is always essential. But one-way conversations go down about as well with most men as they do with most women, and #MeToo isn't going to succeed in the long run if the underlying message is #STFU. Movements that hector and punish rather than educate and reform have a way of inviting derision and reaction.

Every woman, and every thoughtful man, is rooting for #MeToo to succeed, not just by exposing male misbehavior but also by transforming it for the better. It won't get that far if people like Gillibrand and Driver drive its high ideals and current momentum into the ground.

Publicly, We Say #MeToo.
Privately, We Have Misgivings.

OPINION | BY DAPHNE MERKIN | JAN. 5, 2018

YOU CAN BE SURE that this weekend at the Golden Globes, Hollywood celebrities, not exactly known for their independent thinking, will turn the red carpet into a #MeToo moment replete with designer duds. Many have promised to wear black dresses to protest the stream of allegations against industry moguls and actors. Perhaps Meryl Streep will get grilled — again — about what she knew about Harvey Weinstein. The rest of us will diligently follow along on Twitter, sharing hashtags and suitably pious opprobrium.

But privately, I suspect, many of us, including many longstanding feminists, will be rolling our eyes, having had it with the reflexive and unnuanced sense of outrage that has accompanied this cause from its inception, turning a bona fide moment of moral accountability into a series of ad hoc and sometimes unproven accusations.

For many weeks now, the conversation that has been going on in private about this reckoning is radically different from the public one. This is not a good sign, suggesting the sort of social intimidation that is the underside of a culture of political correctness, such as we are increasingly living in.

The women I know — of all ages — have responded by and large with a mixture of slightly horrified excitement (bordering on titillation) as to who will be the next man accused and overt disbelief.

Publicly, they say the right things, expressing approval and joining in the chorus of voices that applaud the takedown of maleficent characters who prey on vulnerable women in the workplace.

In private it's a different story. "Grow up, this is real life," I hear these same feminist friends say. "What ever happened to flirting?" and "What about the women who are the predators?" Some women, including random people I talk to in supermarket lines, have gone so far as to call it an outright witch hunt.

It goes without saying that no one is coming to the defense of heinous sorts, like Kevin Spacey and Matt Lauer. But the trickle-down effect to cases like those of Garrison Keillor, Jonathan Schwartz, Ryan Lizza and Al Franken, in which the accusations are scattered, anonymous or, as far as the public knows, very vague and unspecific, has been troubling.

Perhaps even more troubling is that we seem to be returning to a victimology paradigm for young women, in particular, in which they are perceived to be — and perceive themselves to be — as frail as Victorian housewives.

Consider the fact that the campaign last month against the Met to remove a Balthus painting that shows a young girl in a suggestive light was organized by two young Manhattan feminists. Fortunately, they were unsuccessful. This is the kind of censorship practiced by religious zealots.

HIROKO MASUIKE/THE NEW YORK TIMES

Anna Zuccaro, left, and her sister, Mia Merrill, last month unsuccessfully petitioned the Metropolitan Museum of Art to take down a painting of a young girl by Balthus.

What happened to women's agency? That's what I find myself wondering as I hear story after story of adult women who helplessly acquiesce to sexual demands. I find it especially curious given that a majority of women I know have been in situations in which men have come on to them — at work or otherwise. They have routinely said, "I'm not interested" or "Get your hands off me right now." And they've taken the risk that comes with it.

The fact that such unwelcome advances persist, and often in the office, is, yes, evidence of sexism and the abusive power of the patriarchy. But I don't believe that scattershot, life-destroying denunciations are the way to upend it. In our current climate, to be accused is to be convicted. Due process is nowhere to be found.

And what exactly are men being accused of? What is the difference between harassment and assault and "inappropriate conduct"? There is a disturbing lack of clarity about the terms being thrown around and a lack of distinction regarding what the spectrum of objectionable behavior really is. Shouldn't sexual harassment, for instance, imply a degree of hostility? Is kissing someone in affection, however inappropriately, or showing someone a photo of a nude male torso necessarily predatory behavior?

I think this confusion reflects a deeper ambivalence about how we want and expect people to behave. Expressing sexual interest is inherently messy and, frankly, nonconsensual — one person, typically the man, bites the bullet by expressing interest in the other, typically the woman — whether it happens at work or at a bar. Some are now suggesting that come-ons need to be constricted to a repressive degree. Asking for oral consent before proceeding with a sexual advance seems both innately clumsy and retrograde, like going back to the childhood game of "Mother, May I?" We are witnessing the re-moralization of sex, not via the Judeo-Christian ethos but via a legalistic, corporate consensus.

Stripping sex of eros isn't the solution. Nor is calling out individual offenders, one by one. We need a broader and more thoroughgoing overhaul, one that begins with the way we bring up our sons and daughters.

These are scary times, for women as well as men. There is an inquisitorial whiff in the air, and my particular fear is that in true American fashion, all subtlety and reflection is being lost. Next we'll be torching people for the content of their fantasies.

Catherine Deneuve and Others Denounce the #MeToo Movement

BY VALERIYA SAFRONOVA | JAN. 9, 2018

JUST ONE DAY after Hollywood offered a show of support for the #MeToo movement on the Golden Globes red carpet and stage, a famous actress on the other side of the Atlantic lent her name to a public letter denouncing the movement, as well as its French counterpart, #Balancetonporc, or "Expose Your Pig."

Catherine Deneuve joined more than 100 other Frenchwomen in entertainment, publishing and academic fields Tuesday in the pages of the newspaper Le Monde and on its website in arguing that the two movements, in which women and men have used social media as a forum to describe sexual misconduct, have gone too far by publicly prosecuting private experiences and have created a totalitarian climate.

"Rape is a crime. But insistent or clumsy flirting is not a crime, nor is gallantry a chauvinist aggression," the letter, dated Monday, begins. "As a result of the Weinstein affair, there has been a legitimate realization of the sexual violence women experience, particularly in the workplace, where some men abuse their power. It was necessary. But now this liberation of speech has been turned on its head."

They contend that the #MeToo movement has led to a campaign of public accusations that have placed undeserving people in the same category as sex offenders without giving them a chance to defend themselves. "This expedited justice already has its victims, men prevented from practicing their profession as punishment, forced to resign, etc., while the only thing they did wrong was touching a knee, trying to steal a kiss, or speaking about 'intimate' things at a work dinner, or sending messages with sexual connotations to a woman whose feelings were not mutual," they write. The letter, written in French was translated here by The New York Times.

The passage appears to refer to the some of the names on a growing list of men who have been suspended, fired or forced to resign after having been accused of sexual misconduct in the last several months. One of the arguments the writers make is that instead of empowering women, the #MeToo and #BalanceTonPorc movements instead serve the interests of "the enemies of sexual freedom, of religious extremists, of the worst reactionaries," and of those who believe that women are "'separate' beings, children with the appearance of adults, demanding to be protected." They write that "a woman can, in the same day, lead a professional team and enjoy being the sexual object of a man, without being a 'promiscuous woman,' nor a vile accomplice of patriarchy."

They believe that the scope of the two movements represses sexual expression and freedom. After describing requests from publishers to make male characters "less sexist" and a Swedish bill that will require people to give explicit consent before engaging in sexual activity, the women write, "One more effort and two adults who will want to sleep together will first check, through an app on their phone, a document in which the practices they accept and those they refuse will be duly listed."

They continue, "The philosopher Ruwen Ogien defended the freedom to offend as essential to artistic creation. In the same way, we defend a freedom to bother, indispensable to sexual freedom." Though the writers do not draw clear lines between what constitutes sexual misconduct and what does not, they say that they are "sufficiently far-seeing not to confuse a clumsy come-on and sexual assault."

Translations of the letter were quickly picked up by Twitter on Tuesday, and responses ranged from supportive to hostile. Asia Argento, an actress who accused Harvey Weinstein of raping her, criticized the Frenchwomen's letter on Twitter.

On the other side of the spectrum, Christina Hoff Sommers, who coined the term "victim feminism," tweeted a quote from the letter and her remarks on it.

In France, tens of thousands of stories have landed on social media under the hashtag #Balancetonporc since the journalist Sandra Muller used it in October in a post on Twitter about an inappropriate come-on she received from a French executive.

The multitude of revelations in France has led to discussion of legislative proposals that would fine men for aggressive catcalling or lecherous behavior toward women in public, and lengthen the statute of limitations for cases involving minors. Marlène Schiappa, France's junior minister for gender equality, said that France's parliament would also debate whether to establish a clear age below which a minor cannot consent to a sexual relationship. The decision came after French prosecutors declined to charge a 28-year-old man with rape after he had sex with an 11-year-old girl.

In March, Ms. Deneuve defended Roman Polanski, the director who pleaded guilty in 1977 to having sex with a 13-year-old girl and who was accused by two other women of forcing himself on them when they were under age. While appearing on a French television channel, Ms. Deneuve said, "It's a case that has been dealt with, it's a case that has been judged. There have been agreements between Roman Polanski and this woman."

In concluding the letter, the writers return to the concept of self-victimization and a call for women to accept the pitfalls that come with freedom. "Accidents that can affect a woman's body do not necessarily affect her dignity and must not, as hard as they can be, necessarily make her a perpetual victim," they write. "Because we are not reducible to our bodies. Our inner freedom is inviolable. And this freedom that we cherish is not without risks and responsibilities."

AURELIEN BREEDEN, DEBBIE LEIDERMAN AND PETER LIBBEY CONTRIBUTED TRANSLATION ASSISTANCE.

Catherine Deneuve Apologizes to Victims After Denouncing #MeToo

BY ANNA CODREA-RADO | JAN. 15, 2018

THE FRENCH ACTRESS Catherine Deneuve apologized to victims of sexual violence who decried a letter she signed with more than 100 other Frenchwomen denouncing the #MeToo movement and its French counterpart, #Balancetonporc, or "Expose Your Pig."

In a letter published in the newspaper Libération on Sunday, Ms. Deneuve said that while she stood by the original statement, published in another newspaper, Le Monde, she did not condone sexual abuse or misconduct.

"I'm a free woman and I will remain one," Ms. Deneuve said in the letter to Libération. "I fraternally salute all women victims of odious acts who may have felt aggrieved by the letter in Le Monde. It is to them, and them alone, that I apologize."

Last week's letter, which said that using social media as a forum for sharing experiences of sexual misconduct had gone too far, drew some praise but also international criticism. The signatories argued that the #MeToo movement had caused people who did not deserve to be condemned to face the same consequences as sex offenders.

"Rape is a crime. But insistent or clumsy flirting is not a crime, nor is gallantry a chauvinist aggression," the letter in Le Monde said. It went on to say that in the wake of the Harvey Weinstein allegations, "freedom of speech has been turned on its head."

In her letter to Libération, Ms. Deneuve said that while last week's letter had denounced the #MeToo movement, "Nothing in the text claims that harassment is good."

The sentiment of the statement had been misrepresented by some of her fellow signatories, she said. "Yes, I signed this petition, and yet it seems to me absolutely necessary today to emphasize my disagreement with the way some petitioners individually claim the right to spread themselves across the media, distorting the very spirit of this text," she continued.

The response to the initial letter exposed a sharp cultural divide in France: Supporters argued that the letter had struck a blow against a growing culture of victimhood, while critics contended it showed a lack of support for victims of sexual harassment.

The debate went to the core of what it means to be a feminist in France and exposed tensions and questions about Anglo-American influences on French feminism.

In an Op-Ed for The New York Times, the French journalist Agnès Poirier wrote, "In the past 20 years or so, a new French feminism has emerged — an American import." She said that this style of feminism, which incorporated "anti-men paranoia," had taken "control of #MeToo in France, and this same form of feminism has been very vocal against the Deneuve letter."

In her letter of clarification, Ms. Deneuve addressed criticism of her own position as a feminist. She pointed to a declaration she signed along with 343 other women in 1971, written by the feminist writer Simone de Beauvoir, in which she revealed she had had an abortion when it was still illegal. "I would like to say to conservatives, racists and traditionalists of all kinds who have found it strategic to support me that I am not fooled," she said. "They will have neither my gratitude nor my friendship—on the contrary."

Trump, Saying 'Mere Allegation' Ruins Lives, Appears to Doubt #MeToo Movement

BY MARK LANDLER | FEB. 10, 2018

WASHINGTON — President Trump thrust himself into the national debate over sexual misconduct on Saturday, asserting that "a mere allegation" could destroy the lives of those accused, as his own White House was engulfed by charges of abusive behavior.

Mr. Trump, in an early morning Twitter post, appeared to be defending two of his aides who resigned this past week after facing claims of domestic violence.

"Peoples lives are being shattered and destroyed by a mere allegation," he wrote. "Some are true and some are false. Some are old and some are new. There is no recovery for someone falsely accused — life and career are gone. Is there no such thing any longer as Due Process?"

The statement echoed Mr. Trump's dismissive response to allegations of sexual misconduct or abuse made over decades against male friends, colleagues and, above all, himself.

At a time when charges of sexual harassment and abuse are bringing down famous and powerful men from Hollywood to Washington, Mr. Trump's defiant stance put him at odds with much of the country, and served as a stark reminder of his own troubled history with women.

It also drew an inflamed reaction, as people took to social media to note that Mr. Trump used similar arguments to defend Roy S. Moore, the Republican candidate who lost his bid for an Alabama Senate seat after being accused of child predation, and Bill O'Reilly, the disgraced TV personality who, along with his former employer, Fox News, paid tens of millions of dollars to settle sexual harassment claims.

Mr. Trump, critics noted, has not let due process prevent him from rushing to judgment in other cases. He has avidly promoted conspiracy theories, like those of the birther movement, whipped up his supporters at campaign rallies with chants of "lock her up" about Hillary Clinton, and demanded the death penalty for five young black and Latino men wrongly accused of assaulting and raping a white woman in Central Park.

For the #MeToo movement, which has spread into virtually every corner of American society — redressing a legacy of injustice even as it wrestles with questions like the dangers of a rush to judgment — Mr. Trump's words were sure to make him, yet again, a lightning rod.

His apparent defense of his two aides — Rob Porter, the staff secretary, and David Sorensen, a speechwriter — ran counter to the White House's portrayal of its response to the accusations of emotional and physical abuse leveled against them. Administration officials maintained that they acted decisively in each case.

But it was in keeping with the White House's initially defensive reaction to the charges against Mr. Porter — a messy trail of conflicting statements that has left the West Wing in turmoil, with angry officials pointing fingers at one another.

The White House chief of staff, John F. Kelly, and the press secretary, Sarah Huckabee Sanders, staunchly defended Mr. Porter initially. Ms. Sanders said the president had "full confidence" in his performance, while Mr. Kelly described him as "a man of true integrity and honor."

Yet the allegations against Mr. Porter and Mr. Sorensen were longstanding, well documented, and at least in Mr. Porter's case, known to the White House for months, even as he held one of the West Wing's most sensitive positions, channeling paperwork to the president.

One of Mr. Porter's former wives, Jennifer Willoughby, obtained a restraining order against him, while the other, Colbie Holderness, presented a photograph of herself with a black eye, which she said came from being hit by Mr. Porter while the couple was on vacation in Italy.

The F.B.I. informed the White House of these charges, which held up Mr. Porter's application for a permanent security clearance. Mr. Kelly has told his staff he ordered Mr. Porter to be fired 40 minutes after learning of the charges, an assertion that other officials disputed.

In the case of Mr. Sorensen, his former wife, Jessica Corbett, told F.B.I. agents conducting a background check on her husband that he had run over her foot while driving a car and extinguished a cigarette on her hand during a turbulent two-and-a-half-year marriage.

For his part, Mr. Trump generously praised Mr. Porter, telling reporters on Friday, "He did a very good job when he was in the White House, and we wish him well." The president made no mention of the women Mr. Porter is said to have abused — a point several of the president's critics noted.

"Look again at the photos of the face of Porter's ex-wife after he assaulted her," Representative Ted W. Lieu, a Democrat from California, said on Twitter. "Victims deserve due process as well."

Mr. Trump has a history of coming to the defense of accused men. In addition to Mr. Moore and Mr. O'Reilly, he defended Roger Ailes, the chairman of Fox News, who resigned amid multiple allegations of misconduct; Corey Lewandowski, his former campaign manager, who was charged with battery after grabbing the arm of a female reporter; and Mike Tyson, the boxer who went to jail for raping an 18-year-old beauty queen.

Frequently, Mr. Trump notes that the charges are old, that they might not be true and that the accused has denied them.

"Forty years is a long time," he said of allegations that Mr. Moore had molested girls as young as 14. "He's run eight races, and this has never came up."

In the case of Mr. Lewandowski, he said, "He's a fine person, he's a very good person. And I don't want to destroy a man. If you let him go, you would destroy a man, destroy a family."

Dozens of women have accused Mr. Trump himself of sexual harassment during his years as a real estate developer, reality-TV star and beauty pageant owner. He has consistently denied the charges, often in terms not unlike those he uses in defending other men.

"A lot of things get made up over the years," he said in 2016, responding to an investigation by The New York Times that detailed what multiple women described as lewd comments and unwelcome advances. "I have always treated women with great respect. And women will tell you that."

Mr. Trump's call for due process does reflect a fear shared by others that the #MeToo movement has gained so much momentum that in some cases, men accused of misconduct are being judged too quickly or punished too severely for sexual behavior that falls into a gray area.

Yet Mr. Trump has been quick to judge in other instances. In the 1989 case of the Central Park jogger, Mr. Trump bought a full-page ad in newspapers calling for the five suspects to be given the death penalty. Even after the convictions against the men were dropped 13 years later, Mr. Trump insisted they were guilty.

"You falsely alleged rape by the #CentralParkFive even AFTER they were exonerated, but said nothing about due process for 5 black boys," Cornell William Brooks, a former president of the N.A.A.C.P., said in a tweet. "For 2 white men accused of wife beating, you argue due process. Due process applies to more than @WhiteHouse staff or white men."

To some critics, Mr. Trump's defensive tone on Saturday was less a setback for the #MeToo movement than evidence of its success — a political and social tidal wave crashing on the doorstep of the White House.

"Trump is now tweeting to legitimize domestic violence," said Amy Siskind, who publishes a weekly list on the web of how Mr. Trump is changing the country. "Like months ago when he defended a pedophile. The reason: a guilty conscience and knowing #MeToo is coming for him soon!"

#MeToo and the Marketing of Female Narrative

BY GINIA BELLAFANTE | JAN. 18, 2018

ON MONDAY, Mathilde Krim died. She was a biologist who spoke five languages; who contributed, in her 20s and 30s, to more than a dozen papers on cancer and virology; ran the interferon lab at Memorial Sloan Kettering; served on a team that developed a method for determining sex in utero; smuggled guns to opponents of British rule in Palestine; threw John F. Kennedy's 45th-birthday party at her East Side town-house; married twice, had a daughter and later received the Presidential Medal of Freedom for her historic work in AIDS research and advocacy. At the news of her death, the internet paid relatively little attention.

Instead, by the next morning, the leading conversation among women whose voices are prominent on social media revolved around the story of a young photographer who had a demoralizing sexual encounter with Aziz Ansari, after going out for lobster rolls with him a few months ago. The woman, who used the alias "Grace," recalled the events of the evening, which began with drinks at Mr. Ansari's down-town apartment and ended with recycled jokes and Uber and sorrow, to a writer for an online publication, Babe. We are meant to infer that the comedian's self-regarding erotic misbehavior began the moment he gave his guest a glass of white wine when she wanted red — there's no place for speculating that maybe he just ran out of Syrah.

Grace came to view what happened as assault, even if the facts she presents do not warrant the charge. Mr. Ansari, as he put it in a statement, believed that he had been given every indication that what had transpired between them was consensual. He continued, he said, to support the essential movement toward sexual equilibrium that was upending the old order, and the world appeared willing to let him do it — few people seeming to demand that his distasteful persistence leave him expelled from public life.

Mathilde Krim in 2010.

But the conversation had its own momentum. Writing for the Atlantic, Caitlin Flanagan, whose interrogations of gender are as welcome by young feminists as hymnals are by atheists, was the first to wonder why Grace, pushed beyond her point of interest, had not simply gone home. The reprisals were numerous. Maisha Z. Johnson, a writer and editor whose website highlights her professional commitment "to the power of digital media for social change and healing," for instance, alerted her Facebook followers that Ms. Flanagan was not trustworthy, offering as evidence a piece that appeared in Bitch Media, several years ago, titled: "Douchebag Decree: Caitlin Flanagan, Our First Douchebag All-Star!" The irony trumped the incivility. The piece attacked Ms. Flanagan, in part, for denouncing Helen Gurley Brown, the Cosmopolitan founder, who at the time of the Clarence Thomas hearings in 1991 jovially said, in response to a question about whether anyone on her staff had ever been sexually harassed: "I certainly hope so."

A counterargument to the idea that young women ought to just extricate themselves from sexual situations in which they aren't having any fun soon circulated, maintaining that the culture conditions them to acquiesce, to prioritize the needs of others before their own. "It feels paralyzing to assert ourselves," Jill Filipovic wrote in The Guardian in reaction to all of this. And yet when I look around at millennial women, problems with inhibition or the ability to hang on to a healthy sense of entitlement are not the ones I am quickest to identify.

A few days before the Ansari controversy erupted, some number of young women had taken to eviscerate the writer Katie Roiphe on Twitter, for a piece she was writing for Harper's Magazine, related to the movement against harassment, but still weeks away from publication.

This week, when the HLN television host Ashleigh Banfield called out Babe for the Ansari story, claiming that it threatened to dilute the crucial work of #MeToo and that Grace had merely endured a "bad date," the writer of the piece, Katie Way, 22, lashed out in an email that Ms. Banfield read on air. It called her "a second-wave feminist has-been," who "I'm certain no one under 45 has ever heard of," and went on to ridicule her hair and lipstick. And yet, Ms. Banfield suddenly had a currency she hadn't had in years.

The quiet treatment of Mathilde Krim, when stacked up against the ubiquity of Grace, ultimately reveals a strain of internet sexism that we are all complicit in perpetuating and barely address — the bestowing of outsize rewards, measured in publicity, for certain female narratives over others, for stories that invite judgments and counterjudgments, nearly always about sex and domestic complexity. Just a few days ago, a young writer, Moira Donegan, found herself anointed in the wake of a well-crafted and thoroughly absorbing essay she wrote for The Cut, in which she announced that she was the woman who had created the fabled list meant to steer women away from potentially dangerous men in the media. And yet this kind of success isn't scalable. It is nearly impossible to imagine a similar reception for a 25-year old woman who composed a powerful piece about how she came to believe in the moral necessity of, say, congestion pricing.

In the course of her career, the academic Anne-Marie Slaughter had written two books and countless scholarly articles about foreign policy, but it wasn't until she wrote a cover story in 2012 for The Atlantic — "Why Women Still Can't Have It All," about her decision to leave the State Department and spend more time at home — that she became widely known.

When Joan Rivers died, the internet exploded because we could talk about what kind of feminist her comedy of self-loathing really made her. Mathilde Krim, who fought passionately against stigma and stereotyping and whose work saved tens of thousands of lives, left us with too little ambiguity — and presumably not enough wisdom on hooking up.

CHAPTER 5

What's Next?

Changing a culture of sexual harassment is extremely difficult. Ask Anita Hill, the lawyer who in 1991 accused Supreme Court nominee Clarence Thomas, her supervisor at the Equal Employment Opportunity Commission, at his confirmation hearing of sexual harassment. Mr. Thomas was confirmed and is still a Supreme Court justice. However, the power of the #MeToo movement to promote change is evident on college campuses, in corporate policies and in legislative proposals. Harvard's business school now covers sexual harassment, sexism and the fraternal culture in the workplace. Microsoft made its policies on sexual harassment claims more effective. And the United States, South Korea and France are reviewing their sexual harassment laws.

Dear Men: It's You, Too

OPINION | BY ROXANE GAY | OCT. 19, 2017

STATISTICS ABOUT the scope of sexual violence are always chilling, but even such accountings do little to capture the true breadth and scope of harassment and assault women face. In feminist discourse we talk about rape culture, but the people we most need to reach — the men who are the cause of the problem and the women who feel moved to excuse them — are often resistant to the idea that rape culture even exists.

Women are being hysterical, they say. Women are being humorless. Women are being oversensitive. Women should just dress or behave or feel differently.

Skeptics are willing to perform all kinds of mental acrobatics to avoid facing the very stark realities of living in this world as a woman.

And then, a man like Harvey Weinstein, famous but utterly common, is revealed as a sexual predator. Or, more accurately, the open secret stops being a secret and makes the news. The details are grotesque and absurd (who among us will ever look at a bathrobe the same again?). More women are emboldened and share their own experiences with the predator du jour or another of his ilk. They share these experiences because all of us know that this moment demands our testimony: Here is the burden I have carried. Here is the burden all women have carried.

But we're tired of carrying it. We've done enough. It's time for men to step up.

I confess I am sick of thinking about sexual violence, both personally and publicly. I've talked about and written about and responded to tweets about it for years. I am filthy with the subject, and yet I know this work must be done so that someday we can banish the phrase "rape culture" from our vernacular because it will have become an antiquated concept. I do not dream of utopia, but I do dare to dream of something better than this world we are currently living in.

We are a long way from that better world, in part because so many seemingly well-intentioned people buy into the precepts of rape culture. So many people want to believe there are only a few bad men. So many people want to believe they don't know any bad men. So many people do not realize they are bad men. So many people want to believe sexual harassment is only a Hollywood problem or a Silicon Valley problem when, in fact, sexual harassment happens in every single industry. There is no escaping the inappropriate attentions and intentions of men.

These same people buy into the myth that there are ways women can avoid sexual violence and harassment — if we act nicer or drink less or dress less provocatively or smile or show a little gratitude or, or, or — because boys will be boys, because men are so fragile, so frenzied with sexual need that they cannot simply control themselves and their baser impulses.

Some people insinuate that women themselves can stave off attacks. They insist we can wear modest clothes or be grateful for unconventional looks, or that we can avoid "asking for it" by "presenting all the sensuality and the sexuality," as Donna Karan has said. With each of these betrayals, the burden we all carry grows heavier.

What this reasoning does not grapple with — and it is a perennial rejoinder to discussions of sexual assault and women's vulnerability — is that no one escapes unwanted male attention because they don't meet certain beauty standards or because they don't dress a certain way. They escape because they are lucky.

Sexual violence is about power. There is a sexual component, yes, but mostly it's about someone exerting his or her will over another and deriving pleasure and satisfaction from that exertion. We cannot forget this, or the women and men who have been harassed or assaulted but aren't "conventionally attractive" will be ignored, silenced, or worse, disbelieved.

And then there are the ways that women diminish their experiences as "not that bad." Because it was just a catcall. It was just a man grabbing me. It was just a man shoving me up against a wall. It was just a man raping me. He didn't have a weapon. He stopped following me after 10 blocks. He didn't leave many bruises. He didn't kill me, therefore it is not that bad. Nothing I deal with in this country compares with what women in other parts of the world deal with. We offer up this refrain over and over because that is what we need to tell ourselves, because if we were to face how bad it really is, we might not be able to shoulder the burden for one moment longer.

In the wake of the Weinstein allegations, a list appeared online, an anonymous accounting of men in media who have committed a range of infractions from sleazy DMs to rape. And just as quickly as the list appeared, it disappeared. I saw the list. A couple of people didn't belong on it simply because their behaviors weren't sexual in nature, but some of them were men whose behavior called for a warning and who deserved public shame. Even where I live, outside the media bubble, in a small town in Indiana, I had already heard some of the stories that were shared.

There are a great many open secrets about bad men.

As the list circulated, there was a lot of hand-wringing about libel and the ethics of anonymous disclosure. There was so much concern for the "good men," who, I guess we're supposed to believe, would be harmed by the mere existence of an accounting of alleged bad men. There was concern that the "milder" infractions would be conflated with the more serious ones, as if women lack the capacity for critical thinking and discernment about behaviors that are or are not appropriate in professional contexts. More energy was spent worrying about how men were affected than worrying about the pain women have suffered. Women were not trusted to create a tangible artifact of their experiences so that they might have more to rely upon than the whisper networks women have long cultivated to warn one another about the bad men they encounter.

Meanwhile, there was a hashtag, #metoo — a chorus of women and some men sharing their experiences of sexual harassment and assault. Me too, me too, me too. I thought about participating but I was just too tired. I have nothing more to say about my history of violence beyond saying I have been hurt, almost too many times to count. I have been hurt enough that some terrible things no longer even register as pain.

We already know victims' stories. Women testify about their hurt, publicly and privately, all the time. When this happens, men, in particular, act shocked and surprised that sexual violence is so pervasive because they are afforded the luxury of oblivion. And then they start to panic because not all men are predators and they don't want to be lumped in with the bad men and they make women's pain all about themselves. They choose not to face that enough men are predators that women engage in all sorts of protective behaviors and strategies so that they might stop adding to their testimony. And then there are the men who act so overwhelmed, who ask, "What can I possibly do?"

The answer is simple.

Men can start putting in some of the work women have long done in offering testimony. They can come forward and say "me too" while sharing how they have hurt women in ways great and small. They can testify about how they have cornered women in narrow office hallways or made lewd comments to co-workers or refused to take no for an answer or worn a woman down by guilting her into sex and on and on and on. It would equally be a balm if men spoke up about the times when they witnessed violence or harassment and looked the other way or laughed it off or secretly thought a woman was asking for it. It's time for men to start answering for themselves because women cannot possibly solve this problem they had no hand in creating.

ROXANE GAY (@RGAY), AN ASSOCIATE PROFESSOR AT PURDUE UNIVERSITY, IS THE AUTHOR, MOST RECENTLY, OF "HUNGER" AND A CONTRIBUTING OPINION WRITER.

The #MeToo Stories
We're Not Hearing

OPINION | BY THOMAS CHATTERTON WILLIAMS | DEC. 7, 2017

THIS WEEK Time magazine announced that its person of the year is actually a group of people: "the Silence Breakers" who have courageously outed the alleged sexual predation of powerful men like Harvey Weinstein and Roger Ailes. This is a sign of real progress. The hope is that this continuing national reckoning will lead to a culture in which women are able to flourish without shame or fear.

But if the cases of high-profile men in politics, media and Hollywood are the cases at which the conversation stops, we will have missed a major opportunity to examine what the very worst sexual abuse looks like — and what we might do to stop it.

Perhaps that's why, in the weeks since the accusations of vile (and possibly criminal) behavior of Harvey Weinstein altered the public consciousness, and as our understanding of sexual harassment has expanded to include all manner of merely boorish behavior, some highly influential celebrities of color — Rihanna and LeBron James among them — sought to direct our focus to the case of a 29-year-old black woman named Cyntoia Brown.

The facts of Ms. Brown's life are heart-rending. An elementary school dropout and runaway born with fetal alcohol syndrome, at the age of 16 she found herself living in a Nashville motel with an older pimp called Kut Throat who drugged her, raped her repeatedly and forced her into prostitution.

On Aug. 6, 2004, when she was 16, she shot and killed a 43-year-old john in his home, when the man allegedly reached under his bed. Ms. Brown testified that she believed he was reaching for a weapon and feared for her life. She also took money and two guns from the property before fleeing. A jury rejected her claim of self-defense, finding her guilty of first-degree murder and aggravated robbery.

Ms. Brown was tried as an adult in 2006 and given a life sentence, which she is serving in the Tennessee Prison for Women in Nashville. She will not be eligible for parole until 2055, when she will be 67 years old.

Those who follow the issue of restorative justice have known Ms. Brown's name for years. There is a 2011 documentary, "Me Facing Life," dealing with her predicament, which became a factor in changing the way that Tennessee deals with child prostitution cases. But she only burst into the national consciousness last month when the #FreeCyntoia hashtag went viral. (Rihanna's initial post on Instagram alone received almost two million likes.)

Fortunately, most American women cannot say #MeToo about such a horrific ordeal. But the truth is that there are many more Cyntoia Browns in our midst than we would like to think.

Consider the case of Sara Kruzan. Her father was incarcerated, and a trafficker named George Gilbert Howard, 20 years her senior, began grooming her for sex work when she was just 11 years old. In 1995, at age 17, she killed him and was sentenced to life in prison without parole in California.

Evidence of the abuse she suffered was deemed inadmissible at her trial. Though recent studies estimate that a staggering 86 percent of women in jail have suffered some form of sexual violence, the criminal justice system routinely fails to take this into account.

Twelve years into her sentence, Ms. Kruzan received a break when Human Rights Watch brought national attention to her case, prompting the governor at the time, Arnold Schwarzenegger, to commute her sentence. She was granted parole in 2013.

I recently spoke to Ms. Kruzan and Elizabeth Calvin of Human Rights Watch, who now collaborate to end the use of life sentences without parole for minors. "Sara and Cyntoia are not unique," Ms. Calvin told me. Such abuse, Ms. Kruzan stressed, "is protected by silence."

Ms. Kruzan told me about the case of a woman named Laverne Dejohnette, a Californian serving a life sentence for murder whose story has not gone viral. Ms. Dejohnette's father was a trafficker and her mother was trafficked. Like many women in prison, "Laverne was sexually abused within her family and is a survivor of incest," Ms. Kruzan told me. She was sexually trafficked by her own parents, yet the mitigating factors of her abuse were not taken into account. "These are stories of relentless violence and forgetting," Ms. Calvin said. "Society forgets these people exist."

For all of the women who have had the strength to share their #MeToo stories, there remain so many women in our culture, most of them poor women of color, who lack the resources or opportunities to add their voices to the growing chorus.

Without for a moment diminishing the pain and suffering — whether physical or emotional — of any woman who has now found the voice to speak out against sexism and harassment, for this moment of collective awakening to have a deeper significance, we have to address a very serious question. If ambitious, highly educated, well-compensated women at major news organizations are being harassed and assaulted with impunity, what is happening to poor and working-class black, brown and white women outside the media's glare?

The deeper question may be whether we really want to know. Nietzsche believed the lower you ventured on the social hierarchy, the less suffering mattered. "The curve of human susceptibility to pain seems in fact to take an extraordinary and almost sudden drop as soon as one has passed the upper ten thousand or ten million of the top stratum of culture," he wrote in "On the Genealogy of Morals." Comparing Africans (and laboratory animals) to a representative of the white upper class, he concluded, with some disdain, that all their torment combined "is utterly negligible compared with one painful night of a hysterical bluestocking."

Such talk now seems monstrous, yet a visitor from outer space could be forgiven for thinking that many of us continue to see things this way.

THOMAS CHATTERTON WILLIAMS (@THOMASCHATTWILL) IS A CONTRIBUTING WRITER TO THE NEW YORK TIMES MAGAZINE AND A FELLOW AT THE AMERICAN ACADEMY IN BERLIN.

The Conversation:
Seven Women Discuss Work, Fairness, Sex and Ambition

BY THE NEW YORK TIMES MAGAZINE | DEC. 12, 2017

Amanda Hess is a David Carr fellow at The New York Times, where she writes about internet culture. Anita Hill is a professor of social policy, law and women's and gender studies at Brandeis University. In 1991, she testified in front of the Senate Judiciary Committee during Clarence Thomas's Supreme Court confirmation hearing. Laura Kipnis is a professor at Northwestern University and the author, most recently, of "Unwanted Advances: Sexual Paranoia Comes to Campus." Soledad O'Brien anchors and produces the Hearst Television political-magazine program "Matter of Fact With Soledad O'Brien." She has won three Emmys, among other awards. Lynn Povich is the author of "The Good Girls Revolt," the story of the gender-discrimination complaint that she and other women brought against Newsweek in 1970. She was the editor in chief of Working Woman. Danyel Smith is senior editor of culture at ESPN's The Undefeated. She was the editor of Billboard and the editor in chief of the music magazine Vibe. Moderated by Emily Bazelon, a staff writer for The New York Times Magazine and the Truman Capote fellow at Yale Law School. Hannah Whitaker is a New York–based photographer. She is a frequent contributor to The New York Times Magazine and won an Art Directors Club award for her photo essay "Rise and Shine."

HOW DID WE GET HERE?

Emily Bazelon: Sexual harassment has been clearly against the law since the 1980s. The Supreme Court said in 1986 that employers couldn't let one employee create a hostile work environment for another or base advancement on a quid pro quo for sex. And we had what I might call a kind of mini revolution in the early '90s after Anita's testimony about Clarence Thomas before the Senate Judiciary Committee. Women saw that all-white-and-male array of senators, and there was an uprising. We got mad, and we fought back. More women entered politics, and more engaged in politics. I think a lot of people felt as if we were making progress.

And yet here we are, many years later, and we're having another, bigger moment of reckoning. We're hearing new stories every day about men abusing their power at work in some sexual manner. Some of us are feeling radicalized — there's a sense that a lot more needs to change in a fundamental way. Why is this all happening now?

Anita Hill: After 1991, there were a number of other high-profile Supreme Court decisions on sexual harassment, and many of them were very helpful. But there wasn't a legal consciousness among most people that certain behavior was against the law. Now, some people may know that sexual extortion or abuse in the workplace is illegal, but they may not be convinced that it should be or that they will be punished for such behavior. I would say that in addition to the enormity of the revelations, the media's real engagement in covering this issue today from the front page to the style section to the business section to the sports section is probably why we're having such a great consciousness-raising moment.

Clockwise, from left: Amanda Hess, Anita Hill, Laura Kipnis, Soledad O'Brien, Lynn Povich, Danyel Smith

Soledad O'Brien: It's not always about what's legal. Twenty years ago, young women would come to me and say, "This thing is happening at work," and I felt it essential to tell them what the fallout could be. To say: "Let me explain to you what the H.R. department is about. They work for the company. Their goal is to protect the company's financial interests. Here's what will happen: You will become the person who complained. You'll become a pariah. All of your good reviews will become perfectly average reviews, which will then become bad reviews. And then eventually — not immediately — you will be let go for some reason, if you haven't been worn out and already quit." I've seen it many times.

Laura Kipnis: Here's a historical and political way of looking at the current moment. There have been, roughly speaking, two divergent tendencies in the struggle for women's rights that come together in the issue of workplace harassment, which is why I think this all seems so significant. If you look at the history of feminism, going back to the 19th century, you've got, on the one hand, the struggle for what I'd call civic rights: the right to employment, the right to vote, to enter politics and public life. On the other side, there's the struggle for women to have autonomy over our own bodies, meaning access to birth control, activism around rape, outlawing marital rape and the fight for abortion rights. What we're seeing now is the incomplete successes in both of these areas converging. We've never entirely attained civic equality. We've never entirely attained autonomy over our bodies. Which is why the right not to be sexually harassed in the workplace is the next important frontier in equality for women.

Lynn Povich: Many of us in the second wave of feminists thought that if you put the laws on the books, they would be enforced. So there was some legal consciousness at the time, Anita, that you were testifying. But we then realized that you can't legislate attitude; you can't legislate culture. And I think that's why this is such an amazing turning point.

Amanda Hess: I almost feel like every generation needs to have its moment of public reckoning. I was 6 years old in 1991. I didn't learn about the Clarence Thomas hearings and sexual harassment in high school. Then in college, I definitely had some weird experiences with professors, and boys were terrible, but I didn't have a consciousness about what that might mean for me as a woman in the world. I really felt that when it came to the life of the mind, I was equal to men. When I started in the work force, sexual harassment to me was a dumb video I had to watch. Only once I experienced it did I realize that it was a present phenomenon. I worked in college as a messenger at a law firm, and one of my managers there would make comments about my body and bring me to the office computer to show me porn. I was so surprised and naïve, I guess, that I didn't say anything. I spoke up only after a female manager pulled me aside and asked about him — I guess someone else in the office had complained.

Danyel Smith: It's disheartening to hear Amanda talk about having nothing to look back on. I'm having an amazing career. I don't have a lot to complain about. But if I were to start complaining, sexual harassment and gender discrimination would probably be at the top of the list. As a more junior person, I can remember having problems and going to my boss, and whether it was a sympathetic man or woman, the immediate response was always fear. You can see it on their face. You feel like you've just walked into some kind of haunted house. It's basically, "Girl, why did you come in here with this?"

And then as a leader, man, you always try extremely hard not to be that person. You succeed in not panicking. You listen hard, and with empathy and concern. You try not to let worrying possibilities show on your face. You want to be totally present for that person. But in the past, especially as a younger manager, I've been scared for both of us.

SEX AND DESIRE

Bazelon: Is anyone at this table ready for a rule: No more sex in the workplace?

O'Brien: What is sex in the workplace? Is that the guy who hugs you, and you're like: You know what? I hate when that dude hugs me. Is that the person who tries to peer down your blouse? Or is sex in the office literally your boss saying: "Hey, let's get it on! Close the door."

Povich: We can't ban sex in the workplace. I met my husband at work. I know a lot of people who met their mates at work.

Smith: If you're spending eight, 10, 12 hours a day with people, you're going on the road with people, you're going on location with people, you're going to lunches with people, you're going on work retreats with people, the only time sometimes you're even at home is to go to sleep. For so many people, your whole social life is caught up in your workplace.

Povich: I do think there should be rules about banning relationships between a supervisor and an employee who reports to him or her — and many companies have policies about that. And then you have to talk about power. If there is consent, are we saying consent is not enough? How do you define power? In the cases of Roger Ailes and Harvey Weinstein, they had ultimate power. But what if two people work in different departments, but one person is more powerful than another? Say, a doctor and a nurse's aide? It's complicated.

Hess: I think one of the issues is that you can enter into a relationship consensually with someone who has more power than you. But it's a different thing when you want to exit the relationship — and then it puts you in a bind.

Kipnis: But that's pretty much the reality of life. There are always going be hierarchies in relationships, and there are going to be male-female hierarchies until we someday manage to overcome that situation. I think what's necessary in the meantime is transparency about the power relations, so that the less powerful person is protected if or when things go wrong, as they invariably do when you get together with someone you work with. Been there! In academia, it's actually very common to have couples teaching in the same department, and it's just a matter of course that people don't participate in personnel decisions if they've been romantically involved with the person. I don't see why that can't happen in other kinds of workplaces. I'd rather overdo it on transparency than overregulate our lives and prohibit workplace romances out of some misguided fantasy of universal fairness.

Bazelon: If it's just human that sex is part of the mix in the workplace, what do we do about the reality that some people will benefit as a result, while others get passed over?

Hess: Wait — is being sexy a workplace skill? To me, that's insane. I've never thought of that as something that I should cultivate in order to get ahead.

O'Brien: I think that maybe being sexy is not the right way to put it, but I would say being fun, being a get-along kind of person, laughing at a joke, understanding when someone sends a silly flirty message that you're not automatically offended. There was a guy that I worked with, and he sent me a note, "Let's get a room at the Carlyle." And I had just had a baby, and I was so tired, and I said: "God, I would love a room at the Carlyle. I'll tell you what — I will go and sleep by myself for eight hours." If I had said, "I am offended," that would not have worked. Absolutely not. I'd be perceived as not being a team player. Not fun. "You certainly don't want her on your next project."

Bazelon: When that guy emailed you, did he really mean, Let's go get a room? Like, Let's go have sex?

O'Brien: Do I think he actually meant that? No, I do not. I think he was just being an idiot. That was his ridiculous banter, and here's my ridiculous banter back.

Bazelon: You didn't feel threatened?

O'Brien: Not at all. But he was not hierarchically above me. If my boss had sent me that exact same note, it would have been uncomfortable and problematic. I would have called three girlfriends and read the note to them over the phone to see how I felt about it and to figure out what to do. But that first guy was a peer, and part of navigating the workplace is to know how to come back with snappy repartee so that he would see that I'm fun, I'm not interested and let's move on.

REPORTING AND TRANSPARENCY

Bazelon: Anita, when you came forward to testify in the Senate hearing, there were actually three other women who were prepared to testify that they experienced or could corroborate harassment or unwanted attention from Clarence Thomas. But they were never called as witnesses. Even last year's TV movie about the confirmation hearings collapsed those characters into one woman, reducing the scope of the allegations once more. Your story, a foundational story for us about sexual harassment, has been passed down as a story about one woman, when actually there were these other women who were trying to stand with you. I wonder how you think about that.

Hill: Well, of course I think about it from a selfish point of view — that these were women I didn't know who had experienced or were confided in by someone who had experienced the same kind of behavior with Clarence Thomas that I had and could have added credibility to my testimony. But there was also a bigger concern: Those other three women's voices were being erased. They were being told their voices didn't matter. These were three African-American women, and I do believe that race played a part in the decision not to call them. It also sent the message to anyone else who was out there, who knew, who could have stepped up, that she shouldn't even bother.

What has allowed so many women to come forward recently is hearing other women coming forward. And they have a platform —

social media — to do it. And unfortunately, we know that numbers matter. I just hope that we can get to the point where a woman can come forward on her own and one voice is valued.

Bazelon: I think the current moment has been one of amazing solidarity, where women are coming forward perhaps in part because they're trying to protect one another. I've been looking back on my own younger experiences of not reporting various things that happened to me because I thought: Well, I can handle this. I'll be O.K. That was part of my identity as a feminist — I wanted to think that I could stride on. But now I think about the other women who might have been affected by these men we left in place undisturbed, and I wonder about my own complicity, a word that writers like Rebecca Traister have used.

Hill: And if we're constantly saying, "Oh, I can handle this," how will we really know how much we are injured?

Hess: Minimizing bad behavior is a coping mechanism. It's how you survive. I've heard a lot of women who have come forward say: "I might not make a big deal about this if it's just me. But if I can say something that helps corroborate somebody else's story, then that's valuable."

Povich: I've been thinking about this because one of the things that worked for us at Newsweek when we filed gender-discrimination charges against the magazine in 1970 was that we were 46 women. We talked to one another, and we organized. I get that actresses in Harvey Weinstein's world, they don't work for him; they're looking for a part. But at Fox News or NBC, there were a lot of women. And I assume if somebody's hitting on me, they're hitting on somebody else. And I'm not sure why early on some woman didn't say to a trusted friend, "Ugh, I just went into his office, and this happened." And why they didn't then start to document a pattern of sexual harassment and start to organize as a group of women to say, "This is unacceptable." It seems that many younger women, maybe until now, haven't had that sense of sisterhood or talking to one another as a group that we did during the women's movement.

Hess: Women still talk to one another. The women I know do, anyway. But it doesn't always result in collective action. One of the things that's happened in recent years is that even though women have gained footing in the workplace, workers in general have become less powerful in relation to employers. Unions have weakened, and corporate profits have risen. For the generation of women who entered the work force during the financial crisis, a job and career can feel incredibly tenuous. I think that can contribute to women feeling powerless.

O'Brien: Listen, here's the critical question: Someone sees someone else being harassed. Are they really going to go up against their boss, who likes them just fine? Are they going to put their career on the line? How many times have you been told by H.R. that this conversation is completely confidential, to find it repeated a million times? And then adding to the complication, you don't necessarily know what's going on — maybe she's into it kinda sorta, or maybe she seems to be laughing it off. I just don't know that a bystander is going to really do something that could jeopardize a career. Unless it's her sister, unless it's her best friend, I just don't see that happening.

Smith: It's all well and good to talk about the different ways that women can help one another and report, but I sit here and think, So now the women's friends are responsible for reporting this guy who's out here molesting people? Something that I think gets missed in these conversations, because people are so uncomfortable talking about the actual pain of women, is what it feels like to be in that moment of something happening to you. How hard it is to tell anybody, let alone tell an official of some kind. Lots of people are talking about the men who have lost their jobs — Oh, we're going to miss this anchor or that comedian. But I'm wondering, Who is talking about the women and what we're missing when they change jobs or careers after being harassed or abused? Who's talking about that awful moment of wondering: Should I go forward? Do I have the kind of job where people are going to listen to me? Am I worthy enough? Am I a good witness? Did I do something wrong? Was my skirt too short?

WHO SHOULD BE RESPONSIBLE FOR CHANGE?

Povich: I think it's become clear over the last couple of months that many men feel privileged that they can just invade your space, invade your body. And I do think this is a moment where people have to become conscious that you simply cannot do that.

Bazelon: Will the current wave of consequences, which does seem unprecedented, be the thing that makes men think twice and desist?

O'Brien: I think for some people, for sure. I was having dinner with a business professor, and he was saying that he has completely rethought how he interacts with young women and that now he would never meet with a young woman in his office behind a closed door. So his reaction is, No one will ever be able to say that there was something untoward. I don't think that solves the problem or many of the problems we've been reading about — inappropriate touching or kissing. My argument to him was that there are plenty of ways you can mentor young women and not be alone in your office with them. You can meet with somebody in the cafeteria.

Bazelon: Do you worry about women losing out from boundaries like that?

Smith: I worry about it all the time. I hate to say it, but I've had so many conversations with women I've managed over the years, before they go on the road. So often, they're going alone — to cover a band, to cover an artist. And I've said something to the effect of, "What we're not going to be doing on the road is we're not going to be putting ourselves in any potentially scary situations." What's stymieing and so disheartening is that when you're interviewing somebody, it's very helpful to make constant eye contact and to look super interested in whatever they're saying. But that can be taken the wrong way.

Hess: It's your job to create an intimate relationship with this person —

Smith: I know, and I say: "We're not going be out there giving way too much eye contact. We're not going be out there acting like we want to get laid. We're not going be out there hanging out in the studio till 7 in the morning." It's awful, but I've felt like I've had to say it. Women older than me have said similar things to me.

Kipnis: What about the women who do want to get laid?

Smith: Those are some of my favorite women. And we've all been 26, and we've all been 19. And older! But here's the thing, if you're representing yourself as a professional, I need you to handle yourself in a certain way, and I need to keep you safe. But it is unfair. Those female reporters and critics can't always do the same kind of reporting that men do — the rock 'n' roll reporters, the hip-hop reporters, the ones who tend to get a lot of the acclaim. People say: "Where are the women in rock journalism? Where are the women in hip-hop journalism? Where are the women in pop-music journalism?" Well, they can't always stay out with the men until dawn. They can't always be alone in the darkest corners of backstage, soaking up the best and juiciest atmosphere.

O'Brien: Would you have the same conversation with the men?

Smith: It's a different conversation. I've had the luck and joy of working with guys I trust. A lot of men respect women at work. It happens, and it's wonderful. But in new work relationships, especially freelance relationships, in certain situations, I have had to say, "I'm going to need you to act right." **Kipnis:** I keep going back to this thing about the body, women's bodies as our own property and having sovereignty over them — I think that's a place to start. I know there are already all sorts of harassment codes on the books, but what about a specifically no-touching rule? I think that would be a huge advance in the direction of women having autonomy over our bodies. Because I think women have tolerated way too much touchy-feely stuff for too long. You know what I mean — the ick factor, the guy who's always got his hands on you. I do think the toleration for that sort of thing is changing. Including tolerating all the "I just meant it to be funny" jokey kind of groping.

Bazelon: So do we want a "no touching at work" rule? That is enticingly clear. Or do we lose too much from no touching?

O'Brien: I think that's crazy.

Hess: I do, too.

O'Brien: Literally, when I came in, I hugged two people, right? And kissed them on the cheek. And half the people who are colleagues of mine, if we're going to work on a project and I'm excited to work with them, I would hug them and say, "Oh, my God, I'm so happy to see you."

Kipnis: O.K., but then I think we need better training for women, maybe even starting in high school. We need to teach assertiveness. That used to be on the agenda, standing up to people and saying, "That makes me uncomfortable" or "Please don't touch me."

O'Brien: In the workplace, you say that, and you could lose your job, especially if you're early in your career. Years ago, when I was probably 28, I was at an awards dinner, and a very famous anchor person, whom I had never met, came over to me. And I was in a strapless dress, and he started massaging my shoulders, and I remember thinking: Ugh, why are you touching me? You're not a friend. I do not know you. And I remember thinking, I am just going to smile, say, "Oh, hi!" and twist my body back to talk to everyone at the table. And I did not drop a stitch. My entire goal was to make sure that no one around this table of high-powered people who could advance my career were going to see me thrown at all or were made uncomfortable. If you embarrass a person who has power, they will take it out on you. I believe that.

Hill: For years, we've been talking about strategies for working around a creepy person. There are three ways you could approach the problem of sexual harassment. You can fix the women. You can fix the guys. Or you can change the culture. And I think that really, at this point, what we should be talking about is fixing the guys and changing the culture.

Kipnis: Do we have to choose? Can't it be all three?

Hill: Well, I think if we fix the guys and change the culture, we won't need to fix women.

Kipnis: Good luck.

Smith: Here's why fixing women doesn't work for me. We have a table here full of women who were raised to be strong, to be bold, to move forward in different school and work situations. We are the assertive women. We are the ones who know how to speak for ourselves and to say, "This is what I would like my raise to be; this is where I want to live." There are probably 8,000 academic degrees at this table. Yet we find ourselves in scary situations. How much asserting can you do if someone with power over you in a given situation is using that to intimidate and abuse? There is no amount of fixing. There is no amount of shifting in your seat that you can do. Dudes need to just chill.

O'Brien: The answer is change the culture. Imagine if — back to my scenario when I was 28 years old — someone came over and started massaging my shoulders, and two men at the table who were equal hierarchically said right then and there: "Hey, hey, you can't do that.

Do not touch the young women without their permission."

In our office, if someone says or does something that feels inappropriate, we shut it down immediately. We say: "You cannot do that. That is not how this works." The other thing anyone can do is acknowledge and defuse the situation. If someone had done that at the table, I wouldn't have had to worry about whether that dodge offended anyone. I think women worry about that a lot — Boy, I hope everybody else was comfortable with this thing that was perpetrated upon me.

Povich: I agree that we have to talk about men's role in this — not just the bad men, but all the other men. Many of us are married to, or partnered with, very good men who would never do any of this, but they have a role in a culture that is complicit. The culture of a company or organization comes from the top, so the top people — mostly men — have a responsibility to make their employees feel safe and secure.

Kipnis: I really want to change the culture, and I really want to change men. I just don't think it's going to happen immediately. So I think we need to teach women, and particularly young women, strategies for dealing with the kinds of situations that are going to arise in the workplace, and in the rest of life too. I know from talking to my female students that they're often at a loss about how to deal with the binds they find themselves in, especially in the context of hookup culture. What surprises me is that they often feel unable to say no to guys and just sort of yield instead, even when they don't really want to. Somehow all the messages about assertiveness from the last few generations of feminism have gotten dissipated, and we're back to Square 1.

Hess: I think that freezing and trying to slip away when something upsetting happens to you is a human response. I think it's also a very human response sometimes for people who are witnessing some sort of harassment, even men. I don't think we can necessarily teach that response away.

Hill: One of the things that I think you are saying, Soledad, is that there are big costs for being assertive, for asserting your own person, your own body. Also, I think we have to understand the dynamic. In many cases, when people resist harassment, it becomes a game for the man, and it escalates. And it only gets worse for people. And we have to think about other consequences of being assertive. Retaliation against people who complain of harassment is against the law, even if they don't prevail in their complaints. But retaliation still happens to a majority of people who file harassment claims.

O'Brien: I do think it's important to say that while women need to be aware of the ramifications of speaking up, it's good that so many have stepped forward. Not every unwanted advance can be managed with humor or pushback. Also, I think we can try to create a more respectful workplace by speaking up before things get out of control.

WHERE DO WE GO FROM HERE?

Kipnis: The thing that seems different about this moment — and I feel almost perverse saying this — is that it's corporate bosses and their boards that are playing a major role in effecting cultural change by establishing this new zero-tolerance policy. Sure, maybe it's really a public-relations concern about their brand, or insurance companies trying to limit payouts. But it still gives me optimism, despite its coming from the top down, not the bottom up.

Hill: About a month ago, I spoke to a group of businesspeople about this issue, and they seemed genuinely interested. Yes, part of it was probably a fear of losing money. Reputational risks seemed to motivate their interest in solutions as well. But I think part of it was shame that this was going on in their workplaces. The fact that I was even in the room means something.

Hess: Men are scared right now, which is good. But I think one of the problems in the current workplace is that women feel like when they speak up, either they will be ignored and dismissed — maybe literally — or that they're going to ruin a guy's life. I would like for our workplaces to have a space where women can speak openly and honestly about the culture there — the things that make them feel seriously harassed or assaulted, but also just a little creeped out, or knocked off balance, or diminished — that falls outside the legalistic, bureaucratic, totally intimidating experience of reporting to the H.R. office. There's not always a lot of room for that other kind of conversation.

Bazelon: How should minor infractions be punished? If someone does something on the small scale, do we think he should suffer a long-term or permanent consequence? I realize a lot of people think now isn't the right time to worry about whether men get to come back from being exiled. But when courts of law decide cases, they determine the term of punishment up front. We don't have a clear way to do that in the court of public opinion. And I do worry about lifetime banishment for some people. I also worry about due process.

Povich: There certainly should be a thoughtful investigation and due process.

O'Brien: I think we conflate the many different definitions of sexual harassment — the legal definition, someone's personal interpretation. Some things are legally a crime. Other actions would clearly violate a company's standards: inappropriate language, physically grabbing a woman, pressuring an underling for sex. They are all bad and should be stopped, but I think they deserve different levels of punishment.

Hill: Yes, there are small and large offenses; there are degrees. But I want to put it all in context too. In this room, we are relatively powerful, relatively privileged. And what may be a small thing to us may not be a small thing to a woman who is making minimum wage and working in a place where she has to be nice to harassing co-workers in order to just keep her job. It could be a job where there are 50 other applicants ready to take it, and the woman may have a family to support, so she can't even risk saying anything. If she does say something, and then her bosses decide that the infraction wasn't major and "O.K., let's keep that guy on," then she has to look at that person every day. So I think we have to understand that whatever rules may work for us may not have universal application. Some people are just entirely more vulnerable.

Hess: The behaviors that meet the legal standard for sexual harassment are often really extreme. Way, way lower-level things will drive women out of the workplace that are not even technically illegal. Like, if my boss grabbed my breasts one time, he might not be legally responsible for sexually harassing me. But I would definitely be looking for a new job.

Bazelon: Yes. Sandra Sperino and Suja Thomas, authors of "Unequal: How America's Courts Undermine Discrimination Law," have written about this. They explain that the Supreme Court said — in that landmark 1986 decision — that harassing behavior has to be "severe or pervasive" to count as actionable. Lower courts applying that standard set the bar for meeting it too high. And we're still stuck with that.

Hill: But why does a manager or a C.E.O. or any leader have to wait until something becomes a violation of the law before they act? The law really is just a floor. A company can have its own rules that say: You can't talk about porn or view porn at work, or make jokes about a co-worker's sex life or menstrual cycle, or continue to ask a colleague to date after she's turned you down twice. And if you do, you will get written up; it will go in your file. And if it happens serially, then there are more serious repercussions. You can be fired.

Bazelon: What do we want that we haven't seen yet?

O'Brien: I think it's about opening up more opportunities for reporting.

Bazelon: What would you all think about a reporting system that works like an escrow account? The idea is that when you make a complaint, it stays locked away, and no one acts on it, until someone else makes a complaint about the same harasser. Then the information goes to the authorities. Or you could have a system that alerts the people who made the complaints about other complaints, and they decide what to do. Conor Friedersdorf recently wrote in The Atlantic about this idea, which was proposed by Ian Ayres and Cait Unkovic. A variation of it is already being used at some universities for third-party reporting of campus sexual assault. Imagine a system like that was really trustworthy. Would it be helpful?

Hill: Yes, and some organizations establish ombudspersons within the organization. And companies are relying on independent third parties to investigate claims. This is especially important if the subject of the investigation is particularly powerful, for example in the case of Roger Ailes. Third-party investigators who are truly independent can give people within businesses more confidence in the outcomes.

Bazelon: What about changing leadership? Do we think that if there were just as many women as men in positions of power, or more women, that we would solve this problem?

O'Brien: TV news is full of women. It's not an overwhelmingly male environment. The problem is a lack of leadership — that many of these harassment incidents are open secrets, that everyone in the company is aware that the culture will tolerate bad behavior.

Bazelon: What about more women top executives?

Hess: I don't think it's a silver bullet. There's some research to suggest that even in female-dominated industries, men tend to rise faster and make more money than women do. Women gaining more power in society does not necessarily mean that this specific behavior is going to lessen. Some men are threatened by women in power, and sexual harassment is one way for them to take those women down a peg. It's a way for men to claim physical and personal control over women, even — maybe especially — as they lose their grip over institutional power across the culture.

Smith: I don't know that a world with more women in power would be that different. Women are not a monolith — value systems run the gamut. I will say this, though: Sometimes it seems like the more women have, the more confidently we move in this world, the more we gain, the tougher it is going to get for us.

Hill: Well, we've tried it the other way, with men in the positions of power, making all the decisions about hiring and firing and rules of the office. The stories from #metoo and from thousands of letters and emails I've received suggest that harassment is rampant. We also know that cultures that support harassment are likely to support other forms of discrimination. I've never heard of a harasser who is also an advocate for equal pay or equal hiring or equal promotions. So I think we have to move toward having more women in charge of workplaces, and let's just see if it can be different.

Russell Simmons, R. Kelly, and Why Black Women Can't Say #MeToo

OPINION | BY SHANITA HUBBARD | DEC. 15, 2017

THERE'S AN INTERSECTION in almost every hood that teaches young girls lessons about power, racism and sexism. In the projects, where I grew up, I had to pass it almost every day to get home from school.

This intersection is where some of the guys from the neighborhood would stand around, play music, trash-talk about which artist should hold the title of greatest rapper, and then, suddenly, turn into dangerous predators when young girls walked by. This is where young girls like me learned to shrink into ourselves and remain silent.

On this intersection, like so many others in the world, your body and sense of safety were both up for grabs. On a good day, if you and a girlfriend remained silent, walking past the group of "corner dudes," who were all about 15 years your senior and screaming about what they would do to your 12-year-old body, would be a short-lived experience.

K.L. RICKS

On other days, especially if you were walking alone, things would escalate quickly. One of the men would grab your butt and you would pretend you didn't feel it. Fighting back would make things worse: If you resisted, they would scream at you, curse at you and, in one particular case, attempt to follow you home until you ran inside a store and waited them out. But cross this intersection enough times and such things start to feel normal.

The normalization of predatory behavior manifests itself in many forms. It's not yet clear how the black community will respond to the news that icons like Russell Simmons and Tavis Smiley are among those men who have been accused of sexual misconduct. (Both deny the accusations.) Unlike when the accusations were made against Harvey Weinstein, however, we have yet to see a flood of prominent figures publicly stand with the victims. What is clear is that too many of us still perform mental gymnastics, of the sort deployed during Woody Allen movies, to justify attending R. Kelly concerts, despite years of reports about him victimizing young girls. For some of us, the basis for this cognitive dissonance was established at a very young age.

From my years passing through that intersection, I came to believe — wrongly — that a person can be a victim only if those committing the offenses against her had great power. By any definition, the corner guys had very little power — and they themselves were victims of those who did. They were victims of a type of power that drove through that same intersection, snatched people away from their families and out of the community for decades. This type of power could stop and frisk them, and return to its patrol cars and proceed with its day. On a good day, if these guys were alone and remained silent without resisting, the consequences wouldn't be as severe. A few cops would pull up, pat them down, curse at them, beat them up and scream for them to get off the corner. On other days, especially if the corner guys were in a large group, things could escalate quickly. Sometimes a corner dude wouldn't make it home that night.

This state-sanctioned abuse at the hands of police evoked, and continues to evoke, a community response that literally and figuratively calls for the protection of these young men, and rightfully so. A community is right to fight against over-policing and brutality. It should encourage victims of police violence to speak up and put pressure on local politicians to take a stand.

But when your community fights for those same people who terrorize you, it sends a very complicated and mixed message. Even worse, sometimes the community members fighting back consist of young women who were once the little girls walking home from school doing their best to be invisible in hopes of avoiding what nobody ever called sexual assault. This sends the message that your pain is not a priority. It tells you that perhaps you are not a victim, because those who are harming you are also being harmed and we need to focus our energy on protecting them. After all, their lives are at stake.

#MeToo is triggering memories of that corner that I've tucked away for 20 years because I've been taught there are greater needs in the community. Perhaps this is part of the reason studies indicate only one in 15 African-American women report being raped. We've seen the unchecked power of white men ravish our communities, and we carry the message of "not right now" when it comes to addressing our pain if the offender is black.

Maybe this is why more victims of sexual assault within the hip-hop community have not come forward. Is it possible that black women who work in hip-hop are silent victims, with pain they have been conditioned not to prioritize? I suspect this is true — but I can't say with certainty.

How can these women who live at the proverbial intersection of race and sexism, who grew up crossing that corner, ever be a part of the national #MeToo conversation when they can't be heard in their own community? The intersection of race, class, sexism and power is dangerous, and the most vulnerable women among us must navigate it alone. They are terrorized, then expected to fight for those who terrorized them because a seemingly greater predator is at large. Their faces will never grace the cover of Time magazine, and in some cases their silence will never be broken, if they hold the same false notions of power and victimhood that I once clung to when the cognitive dissonance became too strong.

SHANITA HUBBARD IS AN ADJUNCT PROFESSOR OF CRIMINAL JUSTICE AT NORTHAMPTON COMMUNITY COLLEGE IN PENNSYLVANIA, A WRITER, A SPEAKER AND A SOCIAL JUSTICE ADVOCATE.

Should We Forgive the Men Who Assaulted Us?

OPINION | BY DANIELLE BERRIN | DEC. 22, 2017

FOURTEEN MONTHS AGO, long before #MeToo spawned a movement, I wrote an essay for the Los Angeles Jewish Journal about a disturbing encounter I had with a high-profile Israeli journalist and author.

Ari Shavit was at the height of his fame when I met him at the home of the Israeli-American billionaire Haim Saban, who hosted a party in his honor. Mr. Shavit's book "My Promised Land" was being hailed as a groundbreaking work in its depiction of the Israeli-Palestinian conflict, and most everyone in the Jewish world wanted to hear from him. I seized on the opportunity to arrange an interview.

But when I arrived the following evening in his hotel lobby with a notebook full of questions, he exploited our professional meeting to pursue sex. The assault started with insistent words, but soon he lurched at me, grabbing the back of my head and pulling me toward his mouth. He urged me to come to his room, and when I refused, he pressed harder with the promise that we wouldn't have to have sex, because — wait for it — he just wanted a hug.

I wasn't the only one. Three other women have publicly accused Mr. Shavit of misconduct.

It took me two years to write about the experience, which happened in February 2014, because there were more risks to writing it than to staying silent. But when Donald Trump's "Access Hollywood" tape leaked, it provoked a deep outrage within me.

Everyone close to me warned that if I wrote about Mr. Shavit, it might damage him but it would definitely damage me. So I wrote about what happened but I didn't name him.

Not that it mattered: The Israeli media quickly pounced on the story and within days, Mr. Shavit outed himself. He offered a public apology and resigned his positions at the Israeli news outlets Haaretz and Channel 10.

Of all the abusive men who have been exposed in recent months, Ari Shavit is hardly the worst. But for me, and the other women he has preyed upon, he is the person that comes to mind when we say #MeToo.

So you can imagine how I felt this month when the 92nd Street Y in Manhattan announced that Mr. Shavit would be its featured speaker this spring on the occasion of Yom Ha'atzmaut, Israel's independence day. His comeback didn't last long: The invitation was quickly rescinded after two more women — both students — accused him of louche behavior.

But the crucial questions remain: What are the limits of forgiveness? Not just of Mr. Shavit but of the dozens who have fallen from grace over the past few weeks and who will continue to live among us, whether we like it or not. When does ostracism end and atonement begin? Is there a pathway for an admitted abuser or predator to seek redemption?

In mulling these questions, I've thought often about the religiously mandated walk-of-shame scene in season five of "Game of Thrones," in which Queen Cersei is forced to atone for her sins by walking naked through the streets as an angry mob spits at her and yells "Shame, shame!" I'll admit to a perverse little fantasy in which the Weinsteins of the world are dealt a similar fate. But most of the time, I suppress my baser appetite for retribution. The punitive justice meted out on "Game of Thrones" may be emotionally thrilling, but it does little to promote a framework for building a more just society.

Judaism offers a prescription for restorative rather than punitive justice that I think can provide a template for all of us — not just Jews — in determining what it should take to readmit transgressors into public life. In Judaism, a religion that prizes deeds over faith, atonement is not an easy process. And why should it be? It is designed to effect nothing less than personal transformation. This is why the Hebrew word for "atonement" is "teshuva," or return — as in a return to your higher self, a return to your essential goodness, a return to recognizing your own dignity and the dignity of others.

The repentance process begins with an "accounting of the soul" (heshbon ha'nefesh), an examination of how one has failed or fallen short. God can forgive sins against God, but notably, sins between people can be forgiven only by the aggrieved.

Judaism requires that transgressors seek out those they've hurt and ask forgiveness of each and every person. If rebuffed, the tradition demands the transgressor ask no fewer than three times before moral responsibility is lifted.

In my case, I heard from Mr. Shavit once. In the midst of the media frenzy following publication of my story, he sent an email extending "a deep apology" while also making it clear he had no idea what he was apologizing for. "I sincerely believed that my advances were well received," he wrote. Before I had a chance to respond, Mr. Shavit issued an obtuse and offensive public apology claiming our meeting had elements of "courtship." It did not.

Genuine repentance requires a combination of accountability and sensitivity, selflessness and self-awareness. Men like Mr. Shavit would do well to remember that a true apology would not make excuses or justify bad behavior but would take full responsibility for what went wrong.

While prayer, "tefillah," is also a key component of atonement in Judaism, it is a private, personal affair between human beings and God, so I won't suggest it for everyone. I do believe, however, that prayer is meaningless if not married to moral action.

The third element of true return is "tzedekah," often translated as "charity," but it comes from the Hebrew root of the word "righteousness." Judaism is not alone in reminding us that those who have hurt others can redeem themselves through giving — perhaps the most quantifiable aspect of atonement. A complete rehabilitation should include a commitment of time and money to a cause that uplifts and empowers those in need. Engaging in a reasonable period of community service could help inculcate humility and selflessness in those who once thought only of themselves.

For public figures like Mr. Shavit — not to mention Matt Lauer and Charlie Rose and Mark Halperin and so many more — their giving could directly connect to their work. What if 20 percent of their book proceeds and speaking fees went to organizations that empower vulnerable women? Perhaps some would criticize such a gesture as cynical or opportunistic. I get it. But true forgiveness requires us to set cynicism aside. There's also the fact that such an unofficial policy might reap significant dollars for worthy organizations in need. Had the 92nd Street Y announced Mr. Shavit's appearance as a commitment along these lines, the community might have actually come to the event instead of condemning it.

Mr. Shavit insists that he has undergone a "deep process of self-reflection" and told The Jerusalem Post that this has been "a personal year of reckoning, humility and change." He also expressed his "unequivocal commitment to women, gender equality and tikun olam," the Jewish concept of repairing the world.

I'm not ready to forgive him — at least not yet. Until restitution is made publicly as well as privately, his reckoning rings hollow. But as Judaism reminds me: It is never too late to repair what's been broken.

DANIELLE BERRIN (@DANIELLEBERRIN) IS A SENIOR WRITER AND COLUMNIST AT THE JEWISH JOURNAL.

The #MeToo Moment: What's Next?

BY JESSICA BENNETT | JAN. 5, 2018

SHORTLY AFTER I became gender editor of The New York Times two months ago, the equally-new editor of the website Jezebel, Koa Beck, and I began a series of conversations on WNYC's The Takeaway. Earlier this week, we recorded a segment about our hopes and worries for the #MeToo Moment in 2018.

WNYC, of course — along with The Times — has faced its own reckoning in these roiling months over the alleged misconduct of employees, as well as a swath of debate about the manner in which each of those cases was handled. But that was not the focus of The Takeaway conversation. Rather, it was what comes next for a movement that upended the news cycle, captured the public zeitgeist, and hardly fatigued.

Were we worried about a backlash? (And what exactly was the backlash we were worried about?)

FRANZISKA BARCZYK

Would we see a kind of Mike Pence-ification of working relationships, where men would quite literally wall themselves off from women for fear of crossing a line that seemed to be in motion?

What would happen to after-work social events — or, more importantly, to male-female mentor relationships, something women already struggle to establish?

And at what point would the stories about individual cases turn into larger systemic action?

"The takeaway from this shouldn't be, men and women can't work together," said Ms. Beck.

Since we left the studio, I've jotted down some notes about what I hope for the year ahead. Among them:

• I hope we can shift public focus away from celebrities like Ashley Judd who were abused by celebrities like Harvey Weinstein to women like Suzette Wright, who suffered in silence for years at Ford Motor Co., and the thousands of women who face sexual harassment daily but may not have the means or access to pursue legal cases or media articles. That seems at least part of the goal of "Time's Up," a new campaign put together by a group of powerful Hollywood actors, which includes a $14 million legal defense fund to help working class women.

• I hope we begin to see men and women step up as bystanders, one of the few ways proven effective at combatting workplace harassment and discrimination (and in fact very easy to do!).

• I hope we talk about *culture* as much as we talk about individuals, and recognize that while the Weinsteins of the world are extreme, the messages we learn about sex, and power, and courtship, and consent, are deeply ingrained and start young — and will take far more than a workplace sexual harassment training to unlearn.

• I hope we can have meaningful, nuanced discussions about due process and women's agency. What can someone accused of sexual misconduct reasonably expect, what is fair, and what range of punishments should be considered beyond the abrupt torching of someone's career? As Daphne Merkin put it in a Opinion column this week, "In our current climate, to be accused is to be convicted. Due process is nowhere to be found." How can we talk about the damaging nature of sexual assault as a whole without conflating the Harvey Weinsteins with the Al Frankens?

• I hope we will start seeing what happens when women take over the reins at major institutions, filling in the gaps left by the fallen men who have long shaped our cultural narratives. (At the Today Show, Hoda Kotb is the latest, replacing Matt Lauer as co-host.) We know from research (ahem: I'll plug my own book here, because I spent a year looking at academic studies on the subject) that organizations with more women are more successful, more collaborative, more profitable, and more inclusive. What effect might those women's leadership have on media and culture at large?

• Finally, I hope we'll see a change, or at least a bit of internal scrutiny, in the way we as journalists do our jobs. The Times, for example, has revamped its approach to covering the red carpet for the Golden Globes this weekend — assigning a Pulitzer Prize winning photojournalist, known for his political work, to photograph the event.

The #MeToo Moment: I'm a Straight Man. Now What?

BY DANIEL VICTOR | JAN. 31, 2018

TEN MEN, ranging in age from their 20s to 50s, arranged their chairs in a circle. The only woman in the group, a sex educator who had organized the gathering, promised not to speak.

The event — called "I'm a Straight Male. Now What?"— was branded as a place for men to "unpack aggression" and share "not-so-politically correct thoughts" in the midst of the cultural moment that has become highly politicized. The men who'd shown up — among them a marketer, a journalist, a podcaster and an organizer of sex-play events — were encouraged to say to each other what they were uncomfortable saying publicly about #MeToo. It took place in a small event studio in downtown Manhattan.

"There is a sense that women want us to be talking about it: 'Guys, go figure it out,'" said Bryan Stacy, the co-founder of a sexual health

FRANZISKA BARCZYK

app and one of the event's hosts. He encouraged the participants to tap into their feelings as a way to release any simmering frustration, anger, fear or confusion.

The resulting discussion mirrored the private discussions that I've observed many men, including my friends, having over the past few months.

First, there was an acknowledgment that men are important allies in the #MeToo movement — they have an ability to call out bad behavior when they (we) see it. (Bystander intervention, as my colleague Claire Cain-Miller has written, is one of the few prevention mechanisms that actually works.)

Second, the men wondered how they could participate without being viewed as disingenuous — or elbowing out female voices. They sensed they could do more to help, but didn't know how.

Lastly, they wondered: How should they be assessing their own past behavior in this brave new world?

STEPHANIE KEITH FOR THE NEW YORK TIMES

One man, a former human-resources director, said he was reported for harassment in the '90s — unfairly, he believed — when he told a female colleague that "You were in my dream last night." He didn't mean it sexually, he said.

Another said that while he logically knew that false accusations are rare, he couldn't help but worry that it could happen to him.

Some men said they saw a lot of themselves in Aziz Ansari, the actor who recently was accused in an online article of ignoring the verbal and nonverbal cues of a former date. In the article, she described his behavior as sexual assault. They wondered if and how often they missed those cues themselves.

At times, it seemed the men were seeking validation as much as solutions. As they revisited their own possible missteps and complicity, they said they were wrestling with the distinction between "I am a bad person" and "I made a mistake."

"We're all kind of guilty to an extent," one of the men said.

STEPHANIE KEITH FOR THE NEW YORK TIMES

As the men unloaded, the event's female organizer, who goes by a pseudonym, "Lola Jean," sat silently as promised. She said that while she disagreed with some of what she heard, she felt it was important for men to air their apprehensions — with the goal of better understanding how to address them.

"Ultimately, I believe it's going to be men helping men in order to be better humans, better allies and better advocates," she said.

Sexual Misconduct Spurs New Elections: The #MeToo Races

BY TRIP GABRIEL AND JESS BIDGOOD | FEB. 20, 2018

IN OKLAHOMA, a state senator was charged with sexual battery after a female Uber driver said he tried to kiss her. In California, a state assemblyman was accused of following a lobbyist into a restroom and masturbating in front of her. And in Minnesota, a lobbyist said a state representative repeatedly propositioned her, including by sending a text that read: "Would it frighten you if I said that I was just interested in good times good wine good food and good sex?"

These and other allegations of sexual misconduct led to resignations by nearly a dozen state and federal lawmakers in recent months, setting off a flurry of special elections around the country to fill seats suddenly left open by the #MeToo reckoning.

Yet the candidates running to replace these disgraced men — many of whom are women — are hesitating to put sexual harassment front and center as an issue in their campaigns. In at least eight state legislative and two congressional races, including special elections in Minnesota and Oklahoma that were held last week, the subject has rarely been mentioned in advertisements, rallies or when knocking on doors.

"You get an eye roll and that's it," said Tami Donnally, a Republican running to fill a Florida State Senate seat on April 10 after the resignation last year of Jeff Clements, a powerful Democrat who admitted to an affair with a lobbyist. Ms. Donnally, vice-chairwoman of the Republican Party of Palm Beach County, said voters shrug off the issue: "'Oh well, another one bites the dust, let's move on, tell me what you're interested in.'"

In Minnesota, Karla Bigham, a Democrat who won a special election on Feb. 12 to replace a disgraced member of her own party, found slightly more interest in the issue, though it did not dominate conversations.

"People were well aware of why we were having a special election," Ms. Bigham, who has been a union organizer, said. "They expected a change and I talked about that on the doors in Minnesota — we need a cultural change in the Capitol."

Some candidates said they have hesitated to press the issue because sexual harassment does not weigh as heavily on voters' minds as do other concerns, such as the economy, local issues or their approval or disapproval of President Trump.

In most years, there are scores of special elections around the country to fill vacancies in statehouses and Congress. Most occur after a lawmaker dies or resigns after winning higher office, getting a political appointment or taking a private-sector job.

This year, sudden openings after revelations of sexual misconduct have added to the count, creating a new brand of #MeToo elections.

Two coming special elections are for Congress: a race on March 13 to fill the seat of former Representative Tim Murphy of Pennsylvania, a Republican who reportedly texted a mistress to seek an abortion; and one on April 24 to replace former Representative Trent Franks of Arizona, who asked female staff members to serve as surrogate mothers for him.

In addition, there are special elections to fill statehouse vacancies left by lawmakers accused of sexual harassment or misconduct in six states, including Florida, Kentucky, Mississippi, Oklahoma, and two each in California and Minnesota.

Both parties are closely watching for districts that flip from Republican to Democrat, seeking signs of a rising blue wave leading up to the November midterms (there have been 36 Republican-to-Democratic flips in statehouses since Mr. Trump's election win), but the seats left open over sexual misconduct allegations are not part of that trend so far.

That is because most were in districts that are safely Republican or Democratic, and voters have shown no inclination to punish the party of a lawmaker who quit after accusations of sexual misbehavior.

In Minnesota last week, Jeremy Munson, a Republican, retained a State House seat for his party in a rural district after the resignation of former Representative Tony Cornish. Leading up to the special election, Mr. Cornish campaigned for Mr. Munson. In an interview, Mr. Cornish said, "I didn't run into any negativity in personal appearances or anything else."

Mr. Cornish, a former deputy sheriff of Blue Earth County, stepped down after a lobbyist in the capital, Sarah Walker, said he had propositioned her for years.

Ms. Walker said she viewed it as outrageous that a candidate would want Mr. Cornish's endorsement on the campaign trail. "To me it seems to speak to the Republicans' total disregard or concern about sexual harassment allegations," she said. Another candidate not shying from the support of a fallen legislator is Steve Montenegro of Arizona, who hopes to fill the seat of Mr. Franks, the Republican who was accused of offering an aide $5 million to be a surrogate mother for his baby. Mr. Montenegro, a conservative state senator who resigned to run for the seat, quickly touted an endorsement from the departing congressman. "Trent has asked me to run," Mr. Montenegro said in a Facebook video posted the day Mr. Franks resigned, "and that's an honor."

The Arizona district covers reliably Republican suburbs outside Phoenix, and it is widely expected to remain in Republican hands. State Senator Debbie Lesko, another Republican seeking the seat, said she has largely avoided the subject of Mr. Franks's disgrace, although occasionally it comes up on the trail.

"I usually respond by saying, 'Well, in the Republican primary, it's myself and 11 men running, and I'm not going to sexually harass anyone,'" Ms. Lesko said.

Some of the candidates hoping to replace Raul Bocanegra, a California state assemblyman accused by women of groping or unwanted advances, are closely linked with the movement that ousted him. One accused Mr. Bocanegra, a Democrat, of harassing a co-worker last fall; another declared her candidacy after calling for his resignation last year, but has since decided to run in the general election rather than the special election.

"I think there's definitely a feeling for the people running that it's incumbent for them to bring respectability back to the seat," said Adama Iwu, a lobbyist who helped to organize a campaign against sexual harassment in California politics.

But Dan Schnur, a lecturer in political communications at the University of Southern California, said the issue has not dominated races to replace Mr. Bocanegra or to replace Matt Dababneh, another Democratic lawmaker, who is accused of masturbating in front of a female lobbyist.

"Running against a candidate facing these kind of accusations is a different type of challenge than running to replace one," Mr. Schnur said.

In Oklahoma, a Republican easily held onto a State Senate seat that had been occupied for nearly a decade by Bryce Marlatt, who was arrested last year after his Uber driver accused him of grabbing and kissing her. (He has pleaded not guilty.)

Casey Murdock, a rancher and state representative who won Mr. Marlatt's seat in the heavily Republican district, said voters occasionally told him they were disappointed in Mr. Marlatt. Mr. Murdock said he was skeptical about the Uber driver's accusations. "I still, I don't believe it," he said.

Mr. Murdock's Democratic opponent, Amber Jensen, said that with 32 percent of the vote, she had outperformed expectations for a Democrat running in this rural stretch of northwest Oklahoma. She spoke with voters who grimaced over the allegations against Mr. Marlatt, but said she did not make them a central part of her campaign.

"At the end of the race, we all still have to live in the same town," said Ms. Jensen, who owns a construction company. "But behind the scenes, that is something that drove me forward because — well, because, me, too. I've been victimized before. I'm really tired of men making the decisions for women."

#MeToo Called for an Overhaul. Are Workplaces Really Changing?

BY JODI KANTOR | MARCH 23, 2018

WOMEN HAVE SPOKEN. Men have fallen. Corporations are nervous. But are American workplaces making real progress in curbing sexual harassment?

Five months after allegations against Harvey Weinstein led to the mass baring of past secrets, the focus is turning to the future. Government is stepping up efforts: In Washington, the House of Representatives is preparing to train every worker, down to the most junior intern, and state legislators across the country are proposing ambitious new laws. Corporate boards and investors from Wall Street to Silicon Valley are going on the offensive, probing for problems to avoid being surprised. Entrepreneurs are developing apps and programs to help victims discover if their harassers have targeted others. Women in entertainment, advertising and other industries are demanding fundamental shifts, including more females in leadership roles.

The #MeToo moment has shifted social attitudes, inspired widespread calls for change and resulted in unprecedented accountability. But the revelations about the pervasiveness of harassment — and of the legal and institutional failures to address it — illuminate how tough it will be to extinguish.

"We can't fire our way out of this problem," said Paula Brantner, who runs sexual harassment workshops for nonprofits and businesses, pointing out that removing individual offenders is not enough.

Harassment has flourished in part because structures intended to address it are broken: weak laws that fail to protect women, corporate policies that are narrowly drawn and secret settlements that silence women about abuses. "The reality is, the problem is systemic, and we have to address it at a systemic level," said Rory Gerberg, also a consultant whose clients include technology companies.

Nikkie Parra planned to file a lawsuit over sexual harassment at the Southern California restaurant where she worked as a server. When her boss learned of the plans, she was fired.

Even as dramatic headlines have captured attention, many women say they've seen zero change in their own workplaces. At a Mexican restaurant in Lake Elsinore, Calif., a server named Nikkie Parra fumed through a recent shift as one customer recalled the time he asked her to wrestle his penis, another compared a fold in a bar rag to a vagina and her boss sang, "Nikkie Nikkie Nikkie, can't you see, sometimes those hips just hypnotize me."

She gathered the courage to ask co-workers to join her in a lawsuit. When the boss caught wind of her plans, she was fired. "It felt like hopelessness," she said later. "It felt like this is not going to change. Especially with what's going on in the media and all the celebrities, and this still happens."

Women with wider influence share those anxieties. When Tina Tchen, a lawyer and former chief of staff to Michelle Obama, left the White House, she thought she would quietly restart her legal career focusing on workplace issues. Now she is helping to guide the Time's Up Legal Defense Fund, an initiative that sprang up virtually overnight, spearheaded by women in entertainment, and that faces a critical question: whether the more than $20 million donated so far can fund both immediate legal help for low-income workers like Ms. Parra and a longer-term strategy of filing potential landmark cases.

Ms. Tchen has also been working with organizations that have faced harassment allegations: the Service Employees International Union, which was particularly embarrassed given its mission of protecting workers; and Pixar Animation, where John Lasseter, perhaps the most revered animator since Walt Disney, recently took a leave of absence.

Across industries, Ms. Tchen says she sees plenty of resolve for fighting harassment, but a lack of proven mechanisms. "The tool kit is a little bit bare," she said, explaining that there is no consensus on how to report a repeat offender who goes from job to job, or address more minor infractions with measures short of suspension or firing.

But among some major corporations, a fear-driven shift has begun: Harassment is now considered not just a legal liability, but also a

Tina Tchen, a founding member of Time's Up, spearheaded the initiative's legal defense fund.

serious reputational and business risk. Executives and boards are beginning to look at harassment "the same way you think about other risks to your organization" like security or hacking, said Kaye Foster-Cheek, former head of human resources for Johnson & Johnson and a member of three boards.

It's impossible to tell how many workplaces are increasing their efforts. Many do not want to discuss it publicly, for fear of implying that they didn't do enough in the past. But Microsoft made a bold move in December, eliminating forced confidential arbitration for employees who make sexual harassment claims, saying it didn't want to pressure those women to stay silent. For the first time, the Screen Actors Guild has introduced a clear code of conduct on harassment, detailing prohibited behavior and vowing to protect members. Face-book recently made public its sexual harassment policy, staking the company to those guidelines. New York University banned romantic relationships between faculty members and undergraduates or any-one over whom they exercise "supervisory authority," a move that was already under consideration but that passed after the Weinstein alle-gations. And Seattle enacted new city rules and procedures to ensure respectful behavior on construction sites.

"For the first time I'm seeing a discussion about, 'Even if this behav-ior doesn't rise to the level of legal sexual harassment, we won't toler-ate it,'" said Johnny C. Taylor Jr., president of the Society for Human Resource Management.

In the past, the burden for uncovering misconduct was almost always on victims, but now some companies are assuming a fact-finding role. More are turning to anonymous but detailed employee surveys with questions like "Do you feel safe?" and "Have you experienced harassment?" If workers say yes, the company won't know the partic-ulars, but it can initiate investigations or increase training.

In recent months, Katharine Zaleski, an entrepreneur in New York, has been contacted by two powerful institutional investors, Invesco and Cambridge Associates, that were vetting male venture capitalists whom they were considering funding. They wanted to make sure these men had not behaved problematically, she said. (Invesco declined to com-ment; Cambridge Associates declined to address specifics, but a spokes-woman said in an email, "We take culture, policies and conduct very seriously when we consider managers for our clients' investments.")

More companies are now accepting that "complaint and reporting procedures have failed," said Freada Kapor Klein, who helped estab-lish the field of sexual harassment training and, as an investor, has helped push through changes at Uber and other companies.

Entrepreneurs are developing new systems for women to report their experiences — and for businesses to understand what is trans-piring. TEQuitable, a platform created by Lisa Gelobter and Heidi Williams, connects workers with real-world support and can send com-panies anonymized alerts about complaints. Callisto, which is used on campuses to report sexual assaults, is being adapted for workplace

Lisa Gelobter is co-creator of TEQuitable, a platform that connects workers with support and alerts employers to complaints of harassment within their ranks.

use, said Jess Ladd, the founder. Vault, created by Neta Meidav, helps women save evidence and, like Callisto, shows users if others have named the same offender.

More traditional strategies, like sexual harassment training, are also booming. "I could be booked between now and 10 years from now and still not fulfill the degree of demand," said Stephen Paskoff, a longtime trainer whose clients include Coca-Cola and Verizon Wireless.

But the record on workplace harassment training is mixed. California, Connecticut and Maine have required it for years (New York City may soon join them). Those requirements led to a surge in cheap, off-the-shelf training videos and software that could insulate companies from lawsuits, by demonstrating that they had taken measures to prevent harassment, while actually helping perpetuate the problem, because the tutorials were superficial. After harassment allegations surfaced last fall in the Texas Legislature, leaders promised training and then distributed a rote-sounding video and quiz that drew derision.

The most effective training is expensive, requiring small-group sessions, deep looks at organizational culture and frequent follow-up. But even those who deliver it warn that it is not a complete solution. "Do you think if Harvey Weinstein went to a harassment training class it would have prohibited his behavior?" Mr. Paskoff asked.

And in some cases, the public pressure on companies just means that more quiet financial force is being used. Several employment lawyers say that settlement amounts have been rising. "Cases are settling for premium dollars very quickly," said Debra Katz, a lawyer in Washington, who added that she had settled three cases against chief executives in recent months. Employers are "paying to avoid the public black eye, being outed as harassers," she said. (New Jersey and other states are considering bans or limits on secret settlements, setting up what is likely to be a fight between those who argue that the agreements enable harassment by burying the problem and those who stress that they are often a woman's best recourse.)

In industries like food service and cleaning that have typically offered workers fewer protections, the momentum that has picked up in recent months has no clear outlet. Organizers who work with female janitors, fast food workers, hotel housekeepers, nannies and eldercare providers say that women in those fields have become more willing to speak up. But it's not clear whom they should tell.

Etelbina Hauser, a Honduran immigrant who cleans houses in Seattle, said she felt bolstered by the Hollywood women who spoke out about harassment. "It makes me feel powerful because I feel like all women are joining together," she said in Spanish. Two men have exposed themselves to Ms. Hauser while she was cleaning their homes. A third propositioned her for sex. In each case she fled, gave up the job and essentially kept the experience to herself.

Self-employed workers like Ms. Hauser have no colleagues, no human resources department, no concrete employment policies. "In many cases no one knows this woman is working there," said Ai-jen Poo, executive director of the National Domestic Workers Alliance.

ANNABEL CLARK FOR THE NEW YORK TIMES

For self-employed workers like Etelbina Hauser, who cleans homes in Seattle, there are few structures in place to prevent or report harassment.

When The New York Times asked a number of low-wage employers if they had taken new steps in recent months to prevent harassment, almost none said yes. Some would not comment; others, including Walmart, Target, Sears Holdings, Subway, Costco, Aramark and ABM Industries, said they already had the right policies and procedures in place.

What frustrates advocates, lawyers and activists most are giant holes in the federal laws meant to protect women from harassment. Few of the cases that shocked the court of public opinion in recent months would have been likely to prevail in a real court. The law covers only workplaces with 15 or more employees. The federal statute of limitations for filing a suit can be as short as 180 days. Even when a woman wins her case, damages can be capped at $300,000 — less if she works at a small company. This month, a jury awarded Rosanna Mayo-Coleman, a sugar refinery worker in New York, $13.4 million in a lawsuit against Domino Sugar's parent company, but because of the cap she is likely to collect only a fraction of that.

California legislators are working on what activists hope will be a model for the rest of the country: building up state-level protections for victims of sexual harassment to patch the gaps in the federal rules. One proposed state law extends the statute of limitations. Another specifically defines the business roles it addresses: not just "employer," but also producer, director, investor. Another would make supervisors personally liable for any retaliation. "These are wholesale changes in the law; they are new rights," said Noreen Farrell, executive director of Equal Rights Advocates, an anti-discrimination group helping to push the California bills.

Just this week, Washington State enacted laws to make it easier for women to come forward about harassment, including by prohibiting nondisclosure agreements that prevent them from describing their experiences.

The ultimate solution to sexual harassment, many believe, is having more women in positions of power. Until more women are owners, chief executives and bosses, the dynamic may always be the same:

Renee LaChance, a general contractor in Portland, Ore., took action on an electrician for sexual comments.

a man calling the shots, and a more junior woman afraid to resist or report. (As Time's Up grows, this will be its central focus, a leader of the group said; offshoots in advertising and journalism have been announced, and others in sports, technology and venture capital are forming.)

Several weeks ago, Renee LaChance, a general contractor in Portland, Ore., was discussing a renovation with a male electrician when he unleashed a stream of explicit comments about her breasts.

"Haven't you been paying attention?" she asked him, flabbergasted that all the recent news about harassment had not deterred him.

Her solution was simple. "I'm the person in power in the relationship," she said. "I fired him on the spot."

Glossary

accountable To be responsible for the consequences of one's words or actions.

activist A person who fights for social or political change.

allegation A charge or accusation, often without proof, that a person has done something wrong or illegal.

complicit To be involved with others in wrongful or illegal activity; to passively support an action by not preventing it.

consensual An action done with a person's consent or approval.

empower To give a person agency over his or her thoughts, words and actions.

enabler A person who helps to create an environment in which a person can engage in dysfunctional behavior.

feminist discourse The literature, ideas and discussion of women's rights based on the equality of men and women.

hashtag A keyword or phrase prefaced by the number or pound sign used in social media that creates links to other posts using that word or phrase.

intersectional The overlapping of social identities, such as black and lesbian, which contributes to a person's experiences in society.

mea culpa Latin for "through my fault," it is used as an acknowledgement of one's guilt.

metastasize To grow and replicate, and in a cancerous tumor.

rape culture A society in which sexual assault and sexual abuse are normalized and pervasive.

reckoning A time when a person or society is called upon to account for past actions.

settlement An agreement between two parties to resolve a lawsuit or conflict. This can involve an exchange of money for an agreement to drop charges.

sexual abuse Unwanted sexual behavior by one person to another by force or manipulation.

sexual assault Immediate or short-term sexual behavior forced by one person on another.

sexual harassment Obscene comments, unwanted physical contact of sexual nature, unwanted sexual advances or requests for sexual favors.

sexualize To make sexual something not usually associated with sexuality.

sexual misconduct A broad category of unwanted sexual behavior by force, manipulation or intimidation.

social media Digital platforms, such as Twitter, Facebook and Instagram, through which individuals or groups communicate by posting messages, photos, videos and links.

statement A written or verbalized public announcement detailing a person or group's position on a topic or event.

testimony Formal spoken or written statement in a court of law.

toxic Poisonous, unpleasant or harmful.

tweet A message posted on the social media platform Twitter.

whistleblower A person who reports wrongful or illegal activity by a person or group.

Media Literacy Terms

"Media literacy" refers to the ability to access, understand, critically assess and create media. The following terms are important components of media literacy, and they will help you critically engage with the articles in this title.

angle The aspect of a news story that a journalist focuses on and develops.

attribution The method by which a source is identified or by which facts and information are assigned to the person who provided them.

balance Principle of journalism that both perspectives of an argument should be presented in a fair way.

bias A disposition of prejudice in favor of a certain idea, person or perspective.

caption Identifying copy for a picture; also called a legend or cutline.

column Type of story that is a regular feature, often on a recurring topic, written by the same journalist, generally known as a columnist.

commentary Type of story that is an expression of opinion on recent events by a journalist generally known as a commentator.

credibility The quality of being trustworthy and believable, said of a journalistic source.

editorial An article of opinion or interpretation.

feature story An article designed to entertain as well as to inform.

human interest story Type of story that focuses on individuals and how events or issues affect their life, generally offering a sense of relatability to the reader.

impartiality Principle of journalism that a story should not reflect a journalist's bias and should contain balance.

intention The motive or reason behind something, such as the publication of a news story.

interview story Type of story in which the facts are gathered primarily by interviewing another person or persons.

motive The reason behind something, such as the publication of a news story or a source's perspective on an issue.

news story An article or style of expository writing that reports news, generally in a straightforward fashion and without editorial comment.

op-ed An opinion piece that reflects a prominent journalist's opinion on a topic of interest.

paraphrase The summary of an individual's words, with attribution, rather than a direct quotation of their exact words.

plagiarism An attempt to pass another person's work as one's own without attribution.

quotation The use of an individual's exact words indicated by the use of quotation marks and proper attribution.

reliability The quality of being dependable and accurate, said of a journalistic source.

source The origin of the information reported in journalism.

tone A manner of expression in writing or speech.

Media Literacy Questions

1. The article "The Raw Power of #MeToo" (on page 30) is an example of an op-ed. Identify how Margaret Renkl's attitude, tone and bias help convey her opinion on the topic.

2. What type of story is "Russell Simmons, R. Kelly, and Why Black Women Can't Say #MeToo" (on page 180)? Can you identify another article in this collection that is the same type of story?

3. "The Woman Who Created #MeToo Long Before Hashtags" (on page 34) is an example of an interview. Can you identify skills or techniques used by Sandra E. Garcia to gather information from Tarana Burke?

4. In "Harvey Weinstein Paid Off Sexual Harassment Accusers for Decades" (on page 10), Jodi Kantor and Megan Twohey directly quote actress Ashley Judd. What are the strengths of the use of a direct quote as opposed to paraphrasing? What are its weaknesses?

5. Identify the various sources cited in the article "Trump, Saying 'Mere Allegation' Ruins Lives, Appears to Doubt #MeToo Movement" (on page 144). How does journalist Mark Landler attribute information to each of these sources in his article? How effective are his attributions in helping the reader identify his sources?

6. Identify each of the sources in "The #MeToo Stories We're Not Hearing" (on page 157) as a primary source or a secondary source. Evaluate the reliability and credibility of each source. How does your evaluation of each source change your perspective on this article?

7. Does "Harvey Weinstein's Fall Opens the Floodgates in Hollywood" (on page 23) use multiple sources? What are the strengths of using multiple sources in a journalistic piece? What are the weaknesses of relying heavily on one source/few sources?

8. What is the intention of the article "Matt Damon Draws Rebukes for Comments on the #MeToo Movement" (on page 129)? How effectively does it achieve its intended purpose?

9. Does Nellie Bowles demonstrate the journalistic principle of impartiality in her article "Men at Work Wonder if They Overstepped With Women, Too" (on page 72)? If so, how did she do so? If not, what could she have included to make her article more impartial?

10. Read "#MeToo and the Marketing of Female Narrative" (on page 148). What do you think the author's bias is? Why do you think so?

Citations

All citations in this list are formatted according to the
Modern Language Association's (MLA) style guide.

BOOK CITATION

NEW YORK TIMES EDITORIAL STAFF, THE. *#MeToo: Women Speak Out Against
Sexual Assault*. New York Times Educational Publishing, 2019.

ARTICLE CITATIONS

ASTOR, MAGGIE. "Gymnastics Doctor Who Abused Patients Gets 60 Years for
Child Pornography." *The New York Times*, 8 Dec. 2017, www.nytimes
.com/2017/12/07/sports/larry-nassar-sentence-gymnastics.html.

AUSTEN, IAN, AND CATHERINE PORTER. "In Canada, a 'Perfect Storm' for a #Me-
Too Reckoning." *The New York Times*, 29 Jan. 2018, www.nytimes
.com/2018/01/29/world/canada/metoo-sexual-harassment.html.

BELLAFANTE, GINIA. "#MeToo and the Marketing of Female Narrative." *The
New York Times*, 18 Jan. 2018, www.nytimes.com/2018/01/18/nyregion
/metoo-and-the-marketing-of-female-narrative.html.

BENNETT, JESSICA. "The 'Click' Moment: How the Weinstein Scandal Unleashed a Tsunami." *The New York Times*, 5 Nov. 2017, www.nytimes
.com/2017/11/05/us/sexual-harrasment-weinstein-trump.html.

BENNETT, JESSICA. "THE #METOO MOMENT: WHAT'S NEXT?" *The New York Times*,
5 Jan. 2018, www.nytimes.com/2018/01/05/us/the-metoo-moment-whats-next.html.

BERRIN, DANIELLE. "Should We Forgive the Men Who Assaulted Us?" *The New
York Times*, 22 Dec. 2017, www.nytimes.com/2017/12/22/opinion
/metoo-sexual-assault-forgiveness.html.

BIDGOOD, JESS. "Alabama Women 'Make a Stand' in First Election of the
#MeToo Era." *The New York Times*, 14 Dec. 2017, www.nytimes
.com/2017/12/13/us/alabama-women-doug-jones-metoo.html.

BILEFSKY, DAN, AND ELIAN PELTIER. "France Considers Fines for Catcalls as Wom-
en Speak Out on Harassment." *The New York Times*, 17 Oct. 2017, www.nytimes.
com/2017/10/17/world/europe/france-harassment-twitter-weinstein.html.

BOWLES, NELLIE. "Men at Work Wonder if They Overstepped With Women, Too." *The New York Times*, 10 Nov. 2017, www.nytimes.com/2017/11/10 /business/men-at-work-wonder-sexual-harassment.html.

BROMWICH, JONAH ENGEL. "'The Silence Breakers' Named Time's Person of the Year for 2017." *The New York Times*, 6 Dec. 2017, www.nytimes .com/2017/12/06/business/media/silence-breakers-time-person-of-the -year.html.

BUCKLEY, CARA. "Powerful Hollywood Women Unveil Anti-Harassment Action Plan." *The New York Times*, 1 Jan. 2018, www.nytimes.com/2018/01/01 /movies/times-up-hollywood-women-sexual-harassment.html.

CARON, CHRISTINA. "Matt Damon Draws Rebukes for Comments on the #MeToo Movement." *The New York Times*, 17 Dec. 2017, www.nytimes .com/2017/12/17/arts/matt-damon-metoo-movement.html.

CODREA-RADO, ANNA. "#MeToo Floods Social Media With Stories of Harassment and Assault." *The New York Times*, 16 Oct. 2017, www.nytimes .com/2017/10/16/technology/metoo-twitter-facebook.html.

CODREA-RADO, ANNA. "Catherine Deneuve Apologizes to Victims After Denouncing #MeToo." *The New York Times*, 15 Jan. 2018, www.nytimes .com/2018/01/15/arts/catherine-deneuve-me-too.html.

EDSELL, THOMAS B. "The Politics of #HimToo." *The New York Times*, 14 Dec. 2017, www.nytimes.com/2017/12/14/opinion/democratic-party-sexual -misconduct.html.

FALUDI, SUSAN. "The Patriarchs Are Falling. The Patriarchy Is Stronger Than Ever." *The New York Times*, 28 Dec. 2017, www.nytimes.com/2017/12/28 /opinion/sunday/patriarchy-feminism-metoo.html.

GABRIEL, TRIP, AND JESS BIDGOOD. "Sexual Misconduct Spurs New Elections: The #MeToo Races." *The New York Times*, 20 Feb. 2018, www.nytimes .com/2018/02/20/us/elections-sexual-harassment.html.

GARCIA, SANDRA E. "The Woman Who Created #MeToo Long Before Hashtags." *The New York Times*, 20 Oct. 2017, www.nytimes .com/2017/10/20/us/me-too-movement-tarana-burke.html.

GAY, ROXANE. "Dear Men: It's You, Too." *The New York Times*, 19 Oct. 2017, www.nytimes.com/2017/10/19/opinion/metoo-sexual-harassment-men.html.

GELLES, DAVID, AND CLAIRE CAIN MILLER. "Business Schools Now Teaching #MeToo, N.F.L. Protests and Trump." *The New York Times*, 25 Dec. 2017, www.nytimes.com/2017/12/25/business/mba-business-school-ethics.html.

HAUSER, CHRISTINE. "Larry Nassar Is Sentenced to Another 40 to 125 Years in Prison." *The New York Times*, 5 Feb. 2018, www.nytimes.com/2018/02/05 /sports/larry-nassar-sentencing-hearing.html.

HOROWITZ, JASON. "In Italy, #MeToo Is More Like 'Meh.'" *The New York Times*, 16 Dec. 2017, www.nytimes.com/2017/12/16/world/europe /italy-sexual-harassment.html.

HUBBARD, SHANITA. "Russell Simmons, R. Kelly, and Why Black Women Can't Say #MeToo." *The New York Times*, 15 Dec. 2017, www.nytimes .com/2017/12/15/opinion/russell-simmons-black-women-metoo.html? rref=collection/sectioncollection/opinion-contributors&action= click&contentCollection=contributors&region=stream&module=stream_ unit&version=latest&contentPlacement=38&pgtype=sectionfront.

KANTOR, JODI. "#MeToo Called for an Overhaul. Are Workplaces Really Changing?" *The New York Times*, 23 Mar. 2018, www.nytimes .com/2018/03/23/us/sexual-harassment-workplace-response.html.

KANTOR, JODI, AND MEGAN TWOHEY. "Harvey Weinstein Paid Off Sexual Harassment Accusers for Decades." *The New York Times*, 5 Oct. 2017, www.nytimes.com/2017/10/05/us/harvey-weinstein-harassment -allegations.html?_r=0.

LANDLER, MARK. "Trump, Saying 'Mere Allegation' Ruins Lives, Appears to Doubt #MeToo Movement." *The New York Times*, 10 Feb. 2018, www .nytimes.com/2018/02/10/us/politics/trump-porter-me-too-movement.html.

MACKINNON, CATHARINE A. "#MeToo Has Done What the Law Could Not." *The New York Times*, 5 Feb. 2018, www.nytimes.com/2018/02/04/opinion /metoo-law-legal-system.html.

MERKIN, DAPHNE. "Publicly, We Say #MeToo. Privately, We Have Misgivings." *The New York Times*, 5 Jan. 2018, www.nytimes.com/2018/01/05 /opinion/golden-globes-metoo.html.

THE NEW YORK TIMES. "Mea Culpa. Kinda Sorta." *The New York Times*, 1 Dec. 2017, www.nytimes.com/interactive/2017/12/01/us/harassment -apologies-annotated.html.

THE NEW YORK TIMES MAGAZINE. "The Conversation: Seven Women Discuss Work, Fairness, Sex and Ambition." *The New York Times*, 12 Dec. 2017, www.nytimes.com/2017/12/12/magazine/the-conversation-seven -women-discuss-work-fairness-sex-and-ambition.html.

NORDBERG, JENNY. "Yes, It Happens in Sweden, #Too." *The New York Times*,

15 Dec. 2017, www.nytimes.com/2017/12/15/opinion/sunday/sweden
-sexual-harassment-assault.html.

RENKL, MARGARET. "The Raw Power of #MeToo." *The New York Times*, 20 Oct.
2017, www.nytimes.com/2017/10/19/opinion/the-raw-power-of-metoo.html.

RUBIN, ALISSA J. "'Revolt' in France Against Sexual Harassment Hits Cultural
Resistance." *The New York Times*, 19 Nov. 2017, www.nytimes
.com/2017/11/19/world/europe/france-sexual-harassment.html.

RUTENBERG, JIM, RACHEL ABRAMS, AND MELENA RYZIK. "Harvey Weinstein's
Fall Opens the Floodgates in Hollywood." *The New York Times*, 17 Oct. 2017,
www.nytimes.com/2017/10/16/business/media/harvey-weinsteins
-fall-opens-the-floodgates-in-hollywood.html.

SAFRONOVA, VALERIYA. "Catherine Deneuve and Others Denounce the #MeToo
Movement." *The New York Times*, 10 Jan. 2018, www.nytimes
.com/2018/01/09/movies/catherine-deneuve-and-others-denounce-the
-metoo-movement.html.

SCHREUER, MILAN. "A #MeToo Moment for the European Parliament." *The New
York Times*, 25 Oct. 2017, www.nytimes.com/2017/10/25/world/europe
/european-parliament-weinstein-harassment.html.

SENGUPTA, SOMINI. "The #MeToo Moment: What Happened After Women
Broke the Silence Elsewhere?" *The New York Times*, 22 Dec. 2017,
www.nytimes.com/2017/12/22/us/the-metoo-moment-what-happened
-after-women-broke-the-silence-elsewhere.html.

"STATEMENT FROM HARVEY WEINSTEIN." *The New York Times*, 5 Oct. 2017,
www.nytimes.com/interactive/2017/10/05/us/statement-from-har-
vey-weinstein.html.

STEPHENS, BRET. "When #MeToo Goes Too Far." *The New York Times*, 21 Dec.
2017, www.nytimes.com/2017/12/20/opinion/metoo-damon-too-far.html.

VICTOR, DANIEL. "The #MeToo Moment: I'm a Straight Man. Now What?"
The New York Times, 31 Jan. 2018, www.nytimes.com/2018/01/31/us
/the-metoo-moment-im-a-straight-man-now-what.html.

WILLIAMS, THOMAS CHATTERTON. "The #MeToo Stories We're Not Hearing." *The New York Times*, 7 Dec. 2017, www.nytimes.com/2017/12/07
/opinion/the-metoo-stories-were-not-hearing.html.

WINGFFIELD, NICK, AND JESSICA SILVER-GREENBERG. "Microsoft Moves to End
Secrecy in Sexual Harassment Claims." The New York Times,19 Dec. 2017,
www.nytimes.com/2017/12/19/technology/microsoft-sexual-harassment-
arbitration.html.

Index